El Político

Translation Copyright © M. San Pedro 2024
All rights reserved

ISBN 978-1-945028-58-8 (hardcover)
ISBN 978-1-945028-65-6 (paperback)

First published by St. Vitus Dance

Book design and production assistance by Adam Robinson for Good Book Developers (goodbookdevelopers.com)

Editing by Savannah Crenshaw (linktr.ee/savannahcrenshaw)

Please visit https://StVitus.Dance

"You must compete against the requirements of Heaven and apply yourself, if you wish to compose the Perfect King."

—Baltasar Gracián

El Político

The Perfect King (1640)

Baltasar Gracián

Translated by M. San Pedro

Contents

Preliminary Note		ix
About this Book		x
First Approval		xii
Second Approval		xiii
Dedication		xvi

I	The Perfect King	1
II	How Kings Are Made	7
III	The Vicarious King	19
IV	A King of Virtue	35
V	A King of Capable Capacity	47
VI	A King of Sound Administration	59
VII	A King of Discernment	67
VIII	The Phoenix of Kings	77

Works by Baltasar Gracián	87
About the Translator	89

Preliminary Note

I, M. San Pedro, present a modernized English translation of *El Político (1640)* by Lorenzo Gracián[1] of Huesca, Spain. In order to make the reading of the text contemporary, I chose to offer a modernized edition that is not only faithful to Gracián's original intent but also provides guidance on how to be a Perfect King in our personal lives; by mirroring the great kings of the past so that we can be a living statement of kingship in the present and illustrate the qualities of an ideal leader to those around us. It was of the utmost importance to me that I present a version that preserves the integrity of the original writing, even in its punctuation and spacing, and I am more than certain that this modern English translation will be found insightful, lucid, effective, and, most importantly, inspiring.

---

1   Lorenzo Gracián is the pseudonym under which Baltasar Gracián first began publishing. Only his closest friends, Dr. Juan Francisco Andrés, Don Vincencio Juan de Lastanosa, Dr. Juan Orencio de Lastanosa, and Dr. Don Manuel de Salinas y Lizana, knew of his real identity.

About this Book

Baltasar Gracián's *El Político: The Perfect King (1640)* is a book that highlights the successes of King Fernando the Catholic and other great monarchs, as well as the failures and shortcomings of history's more mediocre and egregious rulers. But more pertinently, it is a work that instructs the reader on how to be the Perfect King in his personal life. Written in the 17th century, this treatise covers topics such as the importance of honesty, the art of vicariousness, the nature of sound administration, and the need for virtue, courage, and discernment.

El Político, the second of Father Gracián's seven masterpieces, is more than just a mere historical account of the Catholic King and other monarchs; it is about how he and the other rulers mentioned within its pages can be used as examples that teach us to be better individuals; it is not just about governing a kingdom effectively, but how to govern ourselves and our families effectively. It is not just a work that condemns the more disgraceful rulers of antiquity, but how, through the study and application of its wisdom, we can avoid committing similar disgraces and condemning ourselves.

In this work, Gracián's writing is didactic, yet his ulterior intentions to teach and instruct are brilliantly disguised. He makes us search for the hidden lessons within these golden pages of wisdom—lessons that are to be used as tools to measure ourselves against the greatness of his teachings in order to reduce our imperfect nature—so that we can be remade into superior men. It is a book that teaches a man how to behave, act, and carry himself like the Perfect

Sovereign because, as Father Gracián reminds us, "little must be lacking to be an imperfect entity, and yet everything must be in surplus for there to be perfection, especially in the most important category, which is that of being a king." And after all, a king is a father; his kingdom is his family, and his authority is Christ, the head of his Christian faith.

May the example provided to us by His Excellency, the Great Catholic King of Aragón, King Fernando II, serve as an example of what a consummate man, diplomat, ruler, and Christian leader looks like. And may we also inculcate in our minds the bravery of those other great and conquering kings from the past, so that their examples can galvanize us against our weaknesses and give us the courage to conquer ourselves in the present; in order to be victorious over life in the same way that they were victorious over their enemies. And may the lessons of those rulers, whom Heaven and history view as disgraceful, serve us as a boundary and as a healthy fear, of the fate that awaits us when we fail at the most important of duties: honoring the Most High with our lives by serving those whom he has entrusted to our protection, guidance, and wisdom.

So raise your *Tizona*,[2] shout "*Santiago!*,"[3] and go forward, to become the Perfect King: Strong, Valiant, Loyal, Just, and, most importantly, Pious.

—M. San Pedro

---

[2] **Tizona was the name of the sword carried by "El Cid" (the Lord and Master), Rodrigo Diaz de Viviar, the greatest knight and ruler of medieval Spain. Today, he is still Spain's celebrated national hero and is seen as the ideal medieval knight. His Tizona is currently on display at the Museum of Burgos.**

[3] **"¡Santiago!" is the Spanish translation of Saint James, Spain's patron saint of war, whose name became the rallying cry of Christian soldiers during the Reconquista of medieval Spain.**

First Approval

From Dr. Pedro de Abella, Professor of Arts at the University of Zaragoza

By commission of Dr. Juan Perat, Canon of the Holy Metropolitan Church of Zaragoza, appointed Vicar General, spiritually by the Heavens and temporally by the most illustrious Reverend Don Pedro Apaolaza, Archbishop of Zaragoza, of the Council of His Majesty. I have read *El Político: The Perfect King (1640)*, which, being reborn in this new memoir, will be able to serve as an example to the greatest monarchs. Let its illustrious author offer it with his curious erudition, admonishing teachings, and prudent politics. There is nothing in him, nor herein, that could tarnish the reputation of a Catholic or offend good morals. I feel this way in Zaragoza, Spain, in the Palace, on November 9, 1640.

—Dr. Pedro de Abella

License:

I give permission for it to be printed. In Zaragoza, Spain, November 12, 1640.

—Dr. Juan Perat, Officer and Vicar General

Second Approval

From Doctor Juan Francisco Andrés to His Excellency, the Duke of Nochera, Lieutenant and Captain General in the Kingdoms of Aragón and Navarre

This treatise eternalizes the memory of His Excellency, of the glorious King Don Fernando, the II of Aragón and the V of Castilla. This brief work of his heroic actions, by Lorenzo Gracián, artificially draws and colors with the ingenious brush of his pen not only the ideas of our great Catholic King but, in different instances and at a distance, the virtues and principles of other rulers. May the village of *Sos del Rey Católico (You Are of the Catholic King)* glory in having birthed him, a village whose happiness could cause envy in many cities. I cannot but thank the author of this learned work very much for having been able to choose patrons from such excellent and advantageous parties, whose prudence is credited with their actions. Together, they have turned this treatise on King Fernando II into a pilgrimage that has been published in France, Flanders, Germany, Poland, and other provinces, leaving their lands enlightened and rich with the experiences and glory of this Spanish trophy. Your Excellency, Don Francisco María Carrafa, Duke of Nochera, has invested yourself in defense of the Catholic religion and even shed blood with your generals. Let the military field tell how many times it saw you leading numerous armies and with the courageous courage that you recognized, by order of the Cardinal-Infante Fernando,[4] the fortifications

---

[4] Cardinal-Infante Fernando was Governor of the Spanish Netherlands, Cardinal of the Holy Catholic Church, Infante of Spain, Infante of Portugal, Archduke of Austria, Archbishop of Toledo, and military commander during the Thirty Years' War; the Duke of Nochera served under his command during this military campaign.

and barracks of the French and discovered their designs. And, having happily executed your duties as a practical soldier, you predicted the attempts of the enemy, which, if your martial vivacity had not foreseen them, might have caused great disorder. Let Vienna, Court of the Emperors of Germany, speak of the times they have seen Your Excellency, the eloquent ambassador, on his dais and canopies. But I will only say that Your Excellency must ennoble with his protection this treatise, *El Político: The Perfect King (1640)* by Lorenzo Gracián, for two reasons: the first, because the Most Noble House of Your Excellency knows how to defend the Most Serene Kings of Aragón. History cannot silence it, nor can its feats be obscured by oblivion, because there is no one who ignores the prudence and courage of its two famous knights, Don Antonio Carrafa and his son Don Diomedes, through whose means the magnanimous, King Don Alfonso, recovered the opulent Kingdom of Naples, and so Your Excellency, The Duke of Nochera, as the successor of such enlightened princes, must defend this work.

The second reason why the author of this political work will find asylum in you is because the Duke of Nochera is a protector of learned men, inheriting this inclination from his blood, and because Italy knows that the Palace of His Excellency Don Fernando Carrafa, your father, was a museum of scholars and famous wise men.

El Político: The Perfect King (1640) deserves that Your Excellency do it the honor of a hero and, as Royal Minister, give him the license he begs, because nothing is found in this book that offends the good customs or the royalties of His Majesty. I feel this way, in Zaragoza, Spain, on November 21 of the year 1640.

—Doctor Juan Francisco Andrés

Sum of Privilege:

Lorenzo Gracián has the privilege to print this book, *El Político: The Perfect King (1640),* for ten years without another person being able to print it without his license, under the penalties contained in the said privilege.

—Dispatched by José Yubero in Zaragoza on November 27, 1640.

Dedication

To His Excellency Don Francisco María Carrafa, the Duke of Nochera and Captain General, in the Kingdoms of Aragón and Navarre[5]

I confidently compare one king to all kings of the past, and I confidently compare one king to all future ones: Don Fernando the Catholic, that great master of diplomacy and of the art of reigning, the greatest oracle of reason in any state.

This will be (Oh most excellent Duke, patron, and my teacher altogether) not so much the body of his history as the soul of his leadership; not a narration of his exploits, but a speech of his successes; the many crises of kings, not the eulogy of a single one, all of which are due to the masterly conversations of Your Excellency, achieved from my observation.

I will comment on some of his real aphorisms: the easiest ones, the accessible ones, the precious ones, the hidden ones, and those who yield themselves to whoever presumes to reach them. I will appreciate certain rules, not political

---

5   Don Francesco María Carrafa, Duke of Nochera, was Viceroy and Captain General of the Kingdoms of Aragón and Navarre. From a noble Neapolitan family, he pursued a military career in the cavalry of the Spanish army, participating in warfare in Tunis alongside the Duke of Osuna in 1611. In 1625, he participated in the siege and surrender of Breda, and he was in command of the Neapolitan cavalry in Lombardy, where five years later he would be appointed field master of the Piedmont and Monferrato regions. Gracián served him as priest, confessor, and advisor during the Catalonian revolt.

paradoxes, and make note of dangerous gambles that violate reason, esteeming safety more than novelty.

I protest that my pen does not encourage the favoritism of flattery, for it has never sought matters so remote, and with that said, I excuse my audacity and sometimes even request more of it, finding myself lucky to have been able to write this work. I confidently say that much history has been eternalized by his royal Catholic hand and even more by his spirit, starting with this treatise. It is twice the oracle: once for the arcanity of its inscription and twice for the depth of its thought.

In it, our Great Catholic King is the envy of Tacitus[6] and Commines,[7] not an object of affection, but a spirit.

—Lorenzo Gracián

---

6   Tacitus was a Roman historian and politician. He is widely regarded as one of the greatest Roman historians by modern scholars.

7   Philippe de Commines was a writer and diplomat in the courts of Burgundy and France. He is considered the first modern writer and the first critical and philosophical historian of modern times.

-I-

The Perfect King

King Fernando the Catholic founded the greatest monarchy to date with regards to religion, government, values, states, and wealth; thus, he is the greatest king in all of history.

There were always great virtues in the founders of empires; every king, to be the first of men, must be the best of men, but to be the first of kings, he must be the greatest of kings.

The elegant pen of Xenophon[8] was destined to record the glories of Cyrus, head of the Persian Empire. But human ignorance could not conceive of a king as great as Cyrus, and his reputation as a historian was damaged because posterity believed that what he had written was not what Cyrus had been, but what a perfect monarch should be.

Romulus[9] was the founder of an empire, which was the child of his own valor; and his successors all partook in his greatness. He became an emperor who could, on the crown of merit, fabricate an empire out of diamonds if he so desired. He was a prodigy of ability and, out of courage, founded

---

8   Xenophon of Athens was a Greek military leader, philosopher, and historian.

9   Romulus was the legendary founder and first king of Rome. Various traditions attribute the establishment of many of Rome's oldest legal, political, religious, and social institutions to him.

the Roman monarchy as extensive in order as in centuries. He was born a king, while others had to be made into one.

The heroic jewels that make up the constitution of these great men are the favors of heavenly destiny and the sovereignty of providence, rather than the merits of one's own vigilance.

Sons of this divine supreme election and brothers in greatness were Constantine the Great and King Charles V, who founded the two Christian empires, one in the East and the other in the West.

Celebrate the centuries who deposited three brilliant jewels in the lands of Spain: the founders of your three Catholic kingdoms, Don García Jiménez de Sobrarbe, ruler of the Kingdom of Navarre; Don Pelayo, founder of the Christian kingdom of Asturias in northern Spain, which survived Moorish hegemony to become the spearhead of the Christian Reconquista; and Don Alonso Enriquez of Portugal, who conquered Santarém and Lisbon from the Muslims and secured Portuguese independence from León.

With courage, kingship is obtained, but with prudence, it is established. Alexander the Great had more than enough bravery to conquer but lacked the sagacity to establish himself; either he was no longer envious that none of his successors would equal him or he was too proud to imagine someone else being capable of ruling so well. Tamerlane filled the East more with his terror than with his dominion, a barbaric comet that, with the ease with which it was forged, was undone,[10] and we saw fate repeat itself in our time with

---

10   "A barbaric comet that, with the ease with which it was forged, was undone." Tamerlane was a Turco-Mongol conqueror in the 14th century who is regarded as one of history's greatest military leaders and strategists. He founded the Timurid Empire in 1370 and successfully conquered southern Russia and parts of India. He caught a cold on the way to China and died suddenly on the journey.

Gustavus Adolphus of Sweden.[11] I do not consider the founder of a monarchy to be the one who gave it any principles, whether perfect or imperfect, but to be the one who established it.

Much of the mighty empire of the Turks is owed to the courageous Ottomans, who started it, but much more still to the conqueror Mehmed,[12] who established it in Constantinople, leaving it as a recognized and expansive military power.

The monarchy of France was planted by Pharamond[13] but was established by Clovis I,[14] who crowned it more with his most Christian virtues than with France's most fragrant lilies.

There is also a great distance between establishing a special and homogeneous kingdom within a province and composing a universal empire of various provinces and nations. With the former, the uniformity of laws and similarities in custom, language, and climate make it easy to unite and separate from strangers. The very seas, mountains, and rivers are to France a natural end and a wall for their conservation. But with the latter, like in the monarchy of Spain, for example, the provinces are many, the kingdoms are different, the

---

11   Gustavus Adolphus was King of Sweden from 1611 to 1632 and is credited with the rise of Sweden as a great European power. During his reign, Sweden became one of the primary military forces in Europe during the Thirty Years' War. He died at the age of 37 in the Battle of Lützen. Gustavus was killed when he became separated from his troops while leading a cavalry charge on his wing.

12   Sultan Mehmed II, at the age of 21, conquered Constantinople, an ancient city in modern-day Turkey that is now known as Istanbul, and brought an end to the Byzantine Empire.

13   Pharamond became the first King of France after the departure of the Romans from Gaul.

14   Clovis I was the first King of the Franks. He united all of the Frankish tribes in France and Germany under one ruler, and to the French people, he is considered the founder of France.

languages are several, the inclinations of the peoples are opposite, and even the climates are different. And so, just as it is necessary for a king to have a great capacity to preserve, he must have an even greater capacity to unite.

Nor is the founding of empires limited to any one remarkable or singular way; rather, the way it is established is a reflection of the capacity and ingenuity of the one trying to establish it. In this way, Caesar transformed the aristocracy into a monarchy, and his virtues were as numerous as his crowns. While the Romans conquered the most and the best of the world, he subdued the Romans. He overpowered many kings and defeated as many senators and generals.

Constantine the Great[15] gave rise to the pontifical monarchy and moved his imperial throne to the east, his victorious weapons becoming an arsenal for the Church. He facilitated the conquest of the whole world under the yoke of the holy faith; if only his successors would have been as great. Ismael Sophi[16] was twice as great, for his valor and for his sagacity, because he founded his empire of Persia not from the ruins of the Ottomans but from his own greatness and perseverance. He refused the life of leisure and instead chose the path of the hero, and by Divine Providence (rightfully favorable to Christianity), he faced the Turkic army and bested it.

---

15   Constantine the Great was the first Roman emperor to profess Christianity. He not only initiated the evolution of the empire into a Christian state but also provided the impetus for a distinctively Christian culture that prepared the way for the growth of Byzantine and Western medieval cultures.

16   Ismail I, also known as Shah Ismail, was the founder of the Safavid dynasty of Iran, ruling as its King of Kings (*Shahanshah*) from 1501 to 1524. His reign is often considered the beginning of modern Iranian history and one of its most vital. Before his accession in 1501, Iran had not existed as a unified country under native Iranian rule but had been controlled by a series of Arab caliphs, Turkic sultans, and Mongol khans.

Cunning has its own way of winning, which is to always take advantage of the occasion. An example of this is Constantinople. After the inconsiderate stubbornness of the Christian kings alternately consumed their forces, exhausted their treasures, and deflowered their armies, the Turks came out refreshed, rose up, and conquered everything without resistance: history tends to make examples of the imprudent, not just chastise them.

The glory of the wise African Kings who knew how to play two hands: one of politics and one of courage. And who can leave out the singular barbarian, Genghis Khan, who conquered the whole East, from Muscovia to the walls of China, leaving to his successors more in commitment than in inheritance.

They were all heads of monarchies, the greatness of their spirits corresponding in each to that of their empire. Few of their successors equaled them, and although they may have advanced in terms of command, none equaled them in terms of valor.

But the clear sun that shines among all of them is the Catholic, King Fernando of Aragón, the Perfect King, in whom the divine has deposited nature's garments (virtues), fortune's favors, and fame's applause. Heaven copied and deposited in him all the best virtues of all the great monarchs to compose an empire that contained all the best of all monarchies. He gathered many crowns into one, and when one world was not enough for his greatness, his ability discovered another for him.[17] He aspired to adorn his forehead with Oriental stones as well as Western pearls, and if he did not achieve it in his days, he taught the way to his successors, and to us by his example: that which cannot be

---
17 A reference to his financing of Christopher Columbus' voyage to the New World.

overcome with strength can be overcome with skill. King Fernando the Catholic, of the heroic lineage of the Kings of Aragón, a land that was always a fertile mother of heroes.

-II-

How Kings Are Made

It helps a lot, or hinders, the pedigree and celebrity of a family. But lineage is the secret philosophy of the Most High and the manifested effects of his Sovereign Providence; some of which are more favorable to one than to others. It seems that these things are inherited—natural properties as well as moral ones—the privileges or ailments of nature and fortune—all of which seem to be passed down generationally.

There are houses that carry happiness and success with them hereditarily, and others unhappiness. The one in Austria has always been very successful, prevailing eternally against all the schemes of its emulators.[18]

That of Valois, on the contrary, in France, has been unfortunate, not forgiving this unhappiness even to the privileged females.[19]

There are other lineages that are very warlike by nature and by liking, such as that of the House of Bourbon, a seminary

---

18   A reference to the House of Habsburg also known as the House of Austria, one of the most prominent and important dynasties in European history.

19   A reference to the House of Valois and its Hundred Years' War with the House of Plantagenet, which is considered a war of succession over the crown of France.

of valiant leaders, whose mixture with that of Austria[20] promises in our Most Serene Prince of Spain, with happiness, the courage to be monarch of the universe. Let his real name, BALTASAR PRINCE[21] be an oracle composed of the four syllables, which gives rise to all the four parts of the world, an omen that his monarchy and fame will occupy them all.

In contrast, the family of the Caesars in Rome was barren of successors, both in quality and in number; this is the ordinary punishment of tyranny.

Sometimes, depending on pedigree, kings take more time to make than others, but, once they are made, the tardiness of the principles and virtues they now possess rewards them with a prodigious excess in progress.

The house of the Kings of Aragón was one of eminent greatness in government. All hand-selected, political, sagacious, warlike, prudent, rare, and the envy of all other kingdoms.

He was born and raised not in leisure or among the delights of the King, Don Juan II, his father, but in the midst of his greatest difficulties.[22] The luminations of his birth were like bombardments of rays from the sun, and the rejoicing of the King's Court only multiplied his triumphant victories.

---

20   A reference to Spain's Queen and King, Queen Elisabeth of France of the House of Bourbon and King Philip IV of the House of Habsburg.

21   Baltasar Carlos was the heir apparent to all the kingdoms, states, and dominions of the Spanish monarchy until his early death at the age of 17 from smallpox. He was the only son of King Philip IV of Spain and Elisabeth of France.

22   A reference to the Navarrese and Catalan Civil War, which King Juan II oversaw until his death.

As a child prince, he found himself surrounded by enemies in the Castle of Girona with Queen Juana Enriquez,[23] his mother, that Castilian Amazon who captained so many armies in Navarre, Aragón, and Catalonia.

On that day, five thousand bullets were fired at the castle against a child and his mother, but, like the phoenix, he emerged triumphant from this fire, and all of these kingdoms that conspired against Fernando, the child, would later find themselves submitting to King Fernando, the man.[24]

From heroic instruction comes a heroic and Perfect King. The good or bad odor of the first liquor that is poured into a vessel lasts for a long time. In the same way an eagle rehearses his generous chick to be king of the birds in the pure rays of the sun, let a prince grow up always looking at the splendor and the bright rays of virtue, honor, and courage.

---

[23] Juana Enriquez, 5th Lady of Casarrubios del Monte, was Queen of Aragón and de facto Queen Consort of Navarre as the wife of King Juan II. She was the Regent of Navarre during the absence of her husband in the Navarrese Civil War and also served as Governor of Catalonia in 1462; and finally, she was Regent of Aragón during the absence of her husband in the Catalonian Civil War between 1465 and 1468.

[24] The Siege of Girona: In 1458, her husband Don Juan II became King of Aragón, and in 1460, her father in Castilla provided her with documentation that Charles of Viana was planning to murder his father. Juana showed the document to her husband, who used it to have his son arrested and imprisoned for treason. But the Catalonians protested against the arrest of Charles, and the king then appointed his wife to negotiate with them. In June of 1461, she made a treaty with Catalonia in which Charles of Viana was appointed his father's governor. Shortly thereafter, however, Charles died, and King Juan then proclaimed his son with Juana Enriquez, Fernando, as heir of Aragón and Governor of Catalonia. Since his son was a minor, he had the queen swear his oath to the Catalonians and act as governor in his place. However, she was accused of having ordered the poisoning of Charles and fled to Girona with Fernando, seeking the protection of the bishop, where they were besieged in the castle until July 1462.

It helped Henry IV of France become a great king, having been transferred from the cradle to the pavilion by the example of his father, King Antoine de Bourbon, King of Navarre. The sandals of the Aragonese, Don Sancho, were more glorious than the amber shoes of other kings, since the latter ended up in disgusting dunghills and the former in majestic timbres.[25]

The boy who would become the famous conqueror Jaime I of Aragón was forsaken by his own father, King Don Pedro II, who hated him even before begetting him and threw him away after he was born;[26] he did not want to be a father and provide him with an education in the most important matters. But Heaven intervened and replaced King Pedro with the valiant Caudillo Count Simón Monforte,[27] who would become his father and tutor together. Some men raise their own children as strangers, while the greatest of men raise a stranger's children as their own.

---

25 Sancho Ramírez was King of Aragón and Navarre. After his father's death fighting the Moors at Graus, the papacy organized three international crusades against Islām which all failed. However, the efforts of King Sancho did not. He reconquered many places using his own resources and by the end of his reign, Aragón began to edge toward the Mediterranean coast. Here, Gracián says that the sandals of King Sancho are worth more than the most expensive shoes of those who failed where he succeeded.

26 Jaime was the son of King Don Pedro II of Aragón and Mary of Montpellier. His father was allied with the heretics against the Christians, and when he was 5 years old, his father was killed in the battle of Muret. Jaime was found and immediately declared heir to his father's kingdom by Count Simon de Montfort, head of the Christian crusaders. Count Simon placed the child and future king under the protection of the Knights Templar at Monzón, where he was cared for and educated until he was old enough to assume his responsibilities as King of Aragón.

27 Count Simón Monforte was a French nobleman and knight. He was head of the Knights of Templar and is considered one of history's greatest military commanders.

Heaven outfitted the boy who would be king and conqueror with the harness, and those tender childish limbs that still did not know how to walk had been creaking in mail and armor since birth. All the great monarchs are brought up in this way: hardship and struggle are the education of heroes.[28]

Alexander grew up surrounded by noise, not of parties and entertainments but of the exploits of his father, King Philip II of Macedon, feeding himself on desire and satiating himself with emulation. He was the son of the greatest king of Greece and a student of the greatest philosopher in the world,[29] and became the first great monarch.

Fernando, as a minor, presided over the Courts of Aragón in Zaragoza, supplying it with the capacity of a man at the age of a child. The persecution of father and son by Prince Don Carlos de Viana taught the former to trust more in Fernando and taught the latter how to unite with his father.

The Roman emperors helped themselves by educating their children about the Caesars of the past in order to instill their greatness in them. And when they could not naturally conceive, they sought them out for adoption. In this way, the wise Emperor Nerva adopted the valiant General Trajan and made a body between them; the former was the head and the latter the arms, dividing the faculties: the prudence of the old father and the courage of the young son.[30]

---

28 Here, Gracián reminds us that God equips men for greatness by surrounding them with hardship and struggle from an early age.

29 A reference to Aristotle, who taught Alexander about medicine, philosophy, morals, religion, logic, and art.

30 Emperor Nerva was a wise and prudent administrator who failed to assert his authority over the Roman army. When a revolt broke out among the Praetorian Guard in October 97, he countered it by adopting Marcus Ulpius Trajanus, otherwise known as Trajan, a young and popular general, as his son.

Why shouldn't nature claim the trust between two strangers for itself?

Paternal love or suspicion is a fatal stumbling block upon which many have been ruined. The Ottoman princes were inmates in the sweet prison of entertainment, from which they never managed to escape.[31] Dionysius,[32] the Second of Sicily, did not aspire to command early, and his suspicion of his uncle Dion led to his own isolation and ultimately his downfall. He was raised to spoil, like so many others, so that when he ruled, many were capable of him. They buried Charles the Inept in France even before he was born; in a sense, he was always a dead king.[33]

All the arts are learned, and in all the mechanical occupations, even the easiest, there should be a time for apprenticeship. "There is nothing more difficult," said the Roman Emperor Diocletian, "than to rule well." A man robs himself of providence, the protective care of God, when he skips this most arduous of tasks.

---

31   Here, Gracián warns against ruining one's children and household with either limitless love or excessive suspicion.

32   Dionysius II of Syracuse was the son of Dionysius the Elder. When his father died, Dionysius, who was at the time thirty years old and completely inexperienced in public affairs, inherited the supreme power and began ruling under the supervision of his uncle, Dion.

Dion, whose disapproval of his nephew's lavishly dissolute lifestyle compelled him to invite his teacher, Plato, to visit Syracuse, attempted to restructure the government to be more moderate. However, under the influence of his uncle's enemies, Dionysius conspired with the historian Philistus and banished Dion, taking complete power. Without his uncle, his rule became increasingly unpopular, as he was mostly incompetent at governing men and commanding soldiers. He would eventually be defeated in battle and sent into exile.

33   Charles III, also known as Charles the Inept, was forced to abdicate his throne during a coup led by his nephew Arnulf of Carinthia in November 887.

To their detriment, some become kings without first learning the art of ruling and without any experience. Nino II found himself suddenly engaged in the difficult rule of a scepter.[34] We saw Childeric, the Frenchman, in the middle of a political ocean, not in milk but in blood and pure gallbladder.[35] The risk is great when the experience is zero. Indeed, Don Sancho II of Portugal conceived horror administratively and, what is worse, distrust of himself. Unable to establish his personal command, the refusal to accept royal authority was widespread, even among his own family, until everything was lost.[36]

Fernando handed over his youth to arduousness and his old age to politics. Heaven requires that a king first devote himself to hardship so that he can perfect himself, conquer life, and, later on, govern well, which is the most important of these tasks.

Ages demand their proper jobs: courage belongs to youth and prudence to old age.

---

34 Adad-nirari II was the first king of Assyria in the Neo-Assyrian period. He led six campaigns against Aramaean intruders from northern Arabia and two against the Babylonians.

35 Childeric II invaded his brother's kingdom and displaced him, becoming the sole king as well as the leader of Neustria and Burgundy. His illegal corporal punishment of the nobleman named Bodilo led to his assassination, along with his wife, Bilichild, and his five-year-old son, Dagobert, while hunting in the Forest of Livery.

36 King Don Sancho II of Portugal proved a capable military commander, but with regard to equally important administrative issues, he was less competent. With his total attention focused on military campaigns, his administration suffered from constant internal disputes. Moreover, the middle class of merchants quarreled frequently with the clergy without any intervention from the king. In 1246, Portuguese nobles invited Sancho's brother, Alfonso, Count of Boulogne, to take the throne. He immediately abdicated his French possessions and marched into Portugal, sending King Sancho into exile in Toledo, Spain.

Arms are exercised in the freshness and fervor of youth with ease and with happiness too; this was the opinion of the distinguished Marqués de Mariñano, pondered on another occasion.

Trajan envied the fact that Alexander had begun to reign at such a young age not because of his ambition for command but because he could not emulate such youth and luck. The younger you are, the easier it is to achieve success and the longer you can enjoy it. Happy events come to an end for many in their golden years; General Pompey lost in old age all that he acquired in his gallant youth.

War and weapons require a grain of temerity that is not bound up and found in maturity; the very considerations of old age stop the verve and cool the daring: the prudent were never great fighters.

The prudence of King Philip quickly put down the sword and the harness.[37] Alexander, with his temerity, conquered more than all the kings put together with their great talent.

And the determined Caesar, the embodiment of perennial strength, triumphed with his great audacity over the great prudence of the Roman Senate.

Youth desires to take up arms; however, its greatest risk is not in war but in its immaturity and its weakness towards the vices of recklessness and negligence, which affect everything.

Old age desires the opposite; it loves peace and from its calmness gives laws, reforms customs, composes the republic, and establishes the empire.

---

37 **King Philip II of Spain, whose wise and considered approach to the conduct of political matters earned him the moniker "the Prudent." Here, Gracián seems to indicate that his prudence is to blame for his numerous defeats in war.**

King Fernando began as the King of Sicily, an illustrious jewel in his great harvest of crowns. He then entered Castilla, Spain,[38] a more arduous undertaking than even that which Hercules undertook when he fought the Hydra with its nine heads.[39] It was only through the crucibles of hardship that Fernando saw the excess of his capacity and the greatness of his courage, and it was then known to all that he would be a political prodigy.

The key to any happy and successful undertaking consists in its beginning and, if I may say so, in getting things right from the start. Because, where the mighty river begins to flow, that is where it continues, and afterwards, it is impossible to change the current.

There exist kings who rule contrary to the principles of success and government. Where this is the case, all the prudence, all the fastidiousness, and all the sagacity is still not enough to overcome the difficult contentions that arise.

At the start of a new undertaking lies the greatest risk of making mistakes, and once one is made, more easily follow.

The man who is today the king of great China began his reign from a strong position and with a superior ability to rule, all to the expectations of his attentive vassals; but the corruption in the bureaucracy and army proved to be too

---

38 Castilla, Spain was a large and powerful state during the Middle Ages and was considered the "heart of Spain."

39 Hercules and the Hydra: The Hydra was a serpent-like monster with nine heads that is often referenced in Greek mythology. He attempted to cut off the heads of the beast but every time one was cut off, two more would grow back in its place. After many attempts at cutting off its heads, he distracted it by firing fiery arrows into the monster's lair. Hercules' nephew then handed him Athena's golden sword which he used to cut off the Hydra's one immortal head.

much for him and spoiled the best king that fame would have eternalized.[40]

The vassals of the dawning sun conceive great hopes, and they always have faith that the one who begins will be better than the one who ends, no matter how good he may have been. Fernando was received at a time when the people desired a great king, and he not only satisfied but fulfilled these well-founded hopes.[41]

He also foresaw that those who wanted him to be King of Castilla did not do so because they believed he was worthy of command, but because they had hidden personal ambitions and believed that he could help them further. Feeding them with their own deceptions, he took advantage of the situation and later revolted against them, and, defeating both of them, he was crowned king, king.[42]

---

40   Chongzhen was the 16th and final Emperor of China. Though in a position to save the Ming Dynasty and have fame eternalize his name, his attempts to end widespread corruption and take command of the army failed, and with the treasury depleted and innumerous rebellions taking place, his short reign ended when he committed suicide a few years after this book was written.

41   Here, Gracián subtly mentions Enrique IV of Castilla, also known as Henry the Impotent. At a time when the Spanish Monarchies were disunited and the weakest of all crowns was that of Castilla, the people desired a strong monarch. When King Enrique died, the War of the Castilian Succession ensued. The civil war saw Fernando, the Heir to the Crown of Aragón and husband to Isabella, the half-sister of Enrique, at war with Joanna of Castilla, his purported daughter.

42   Some of the Castilian nobility supported Joanna and Fernando at the same time, in hopes of ultimately siding with whoever the victor was. So Fernando moved to secure the support of Castilla's most powerful nobles: the powerful Mendoza family, the Manrique de Lara family, the Duke of Medina Sidonia, Beltrán de la Cueva, and the Knights of the Order of Santiago and of the Order of Calatrava. Defeating the rest of the nobility and Joanna, he became "king, king": King of Aragón and King of Castilla.

Fernando esteemed the opinions of King Don Juan, his father, and it would be wise for one to esteem them as well; make certain that patience and prudence always prevail, rather than the common inclinations of your nature.

-III-
The Vicarious King

Kings have a notable propensity, for better or worse, to follow the exact opposite of the past, either because of novelty or emulation, and this passion reigns not only in strange successors but also in their own children, for nature can unite bloodlines but not acumen; you can inherit a kingdom but never the greatness of your predecessor. And so, the Perfect King must correctly measure the substance of the men who came before him; his success or failure depends on it, and this measure should be taken in the company of piety and discernment.

For Emperor Vespasian[43] to abhor and erase the traces of Emperor Vitellius and the other monstrosities that preceded him was to restore the empire and to make amends for virtue.

But for Hadrian to condemn the enlightened deeds of Trajan, the best emperor Rome adored, and reach such an extent of disagreement that he narrowed the terms of the

---
43   **Vespasian was a Roman emperor whose fiscal reforms and consolidation of the empire made his reign one of political stability and funded a vast Roman building program that included the Temple of Peace, the Colosseum, and the restoration of the capitol.**

Empire to make himself famous,[44] and demolished Trajan's celebrated bridge[45] in order to demolish his memory, is not emulation but atrocity.

To approve of everything is ignorance; to disapprove of everything is malice; that, because the past king was a warrior, his successor must necessarily be peaceful, is not something born out of convenience but out of malicious opposition. This is neither a wise policy nor a rule that one should govern by.

The evil is that, in what is good and heroic, the majority of kings have imitation as an imperfection; rather than imitate virtue, they imitate vice, and in this, they all battle with each other in fierce competition. The inglorious rulers are many, and they are chained to the dishonorable, while the heroic ones are rare and singular. A depraved Tiberius is succeeded by a detestable Caligula, who is succeeded by an incapable Claudius, and Claudius is succeeded by a perverse Nero. It is such a bewilderment how the nefarious bond themselves to one another, like a regiment of troops; but an Augustus, a Trajan, a Theodosius—men like these—people soon lose sight of, and there is no one who continues to imitate them.

Heaven intervened and matched two monarchies equal in greatness—reciprocal happiness on the part of Fernando to marry a monarch equal to his capacity and value—and, on behalf of Isabella, to obtain a husband blessed with equal eminence and power.

---

44   As emperor, Hadrian broke with the expansionist policies of his predecessors to focus on securing the Roman Empire within its existing borders. Gracián questions his intentions for doing so.

45   Trajan's Bridge, also known as the Danube Bridge, was one of the greatest achievements in Roman architecture and lasted 165 years. The wooden superstructure of the bridge was dismantled by Hadrian, presumably in order to protect the empire from barbarian invasions from the north; although, here again, Gracián questions his motives.

To a small plant, any small vase is a spacious field, but a giant tree, a steep palm, or a towering cedar would find itself violated in such a narrow pot: with no space to grow, they cannot find their range and, thus, cannot not grow to the heights that nature intended. For a king, being equally yoked is a necessary ingredient for success.[46]

If fortune had favored Carlos Manuel de Saboya with better timing, he could have sought an empire as big as his generous spirit and would have even left the great Caesar behind; his spirit was too exceptional and thunderous to be married to the smallness of such a tiny state, and so, sadly, from the sun that could have been, he was relegated to a small star instead.[47]

It is an insufferable torment to a heroic spirit to see that the forces of his kingdom do not reach those of his valor and great luck not to have to envy any foreign monarchy.

Perhaps Henry IV of France coveted the courage of the Spaniards.[48]

---

46 You should be partnered with people who match your capabilities, so you do not find yourself being hindered by those less capable than you.

47 Carlos Manuel de Saboya, known as "the Great," was the Duke of Savoy. A skilled soldier and shrewd politician, he was a capable sovereign, governing with moderation, promoting commercial development, and making his court the center of culture. He sought to turn the state of Savoy into a kingdom but was never able to, as he ruled at a time when both Spain and France commanded most of Europe. Here, Gracián blames fortune and bad timing for being against the Duke. To turn Savoy into a Kingdom would have meant going to war with Spain and France, Europe's two superpowers at the time.

48 Henry IV made many concessions to the Protestants in his attempt to end the religious war that was plaguing France. Gracián seems to wonder if he yearned for and sometimes envied the courage of the Spanish, who rejected Protestantism completely and embraced Catholicism wholeheartedly. Still, he is considered a good king and known as "Henry the Great."

Great unhappiness results when a kingdom is married to a king who lacks quality and power and who does not have a greatness in him that is equal to his kingdom. This was the case with Vladislaus II of Poland, whom history has dismissed as incapable, and Favila of Spain (also known as Favila of Asturias), whom history regards as frivolous. A discredited king is neither desired by his vassals nor feared by his opponents. Great and difficult monarchies ask for kings great in capacity and courage, because the greater his capacity, the greater he will champion his kingdom. The valiant Charles of Burgundy owed nothing to the great Emperor Julius Caesar, and the great Cosmas of Florence owed nothing to the great Octavian, for they were all celebrated for being great men and even greater rulers.

Although it is always dangerous and can lead to ruin when a king is a naturally gifted ruler but inexperienced due to his age, as was the case with Arcadius,[49] there is always hope. But when he is not naturally blessed with the ability to rule because nature has forgotten him, as was the case with the Greek Alexios IV,[50] there is always despair, regardless of age.

It is great luck to be matched equally—the greatness of a ruler with the greatness of a kingdom—but like the lineage of a marriage, this depends on the divine. And when there is no equality, it is better for the king to sin by exceeding the monarchy in greatness than vice versa; but he must be careful not to be dismissive, because that cost Caesar his life.

---

49 Arcadius is historically considered to have been a gifted but weak ruler because of his inexperience; his reign, which began at the age of 17, was dominated by a series of powerful ministers and by his wife, Aelia Eudoxia.

50 Alexios IV regained control of his rights to the Byzantine throne with the help of the Fourth Crusade but was deposed soon after by a palace coup.

Fernando's hereditary kingdoms of Aragón seemed too narrow for his extensive desires, and so he always longed for the greatness and breadth of Castilla, and from there the monarchy of all Spain, and even the universal monarchy of both the old and new worlds.

He reigned in a growing empire, which greatly helps the plausibility of a monarch. How greatly a king is admired depends a lot on the health of his kingdom, which requires that it go from reigning in its expansionism to later reigning in its protectionism.

A fresh and vigorous king engenders the virtues of robustness and strength in his children, but an old king, deprived of his former strength, lacking his native warmth, and surrounded by ailments, produces a frail and weak kingdom.

Great kings all had commonly distinguished monarchies because they were helped in every way to attain the virtues of robustness, strength, wisdom, courage, justice, and temperance by their predecessors: a valiant Romulus gave us a tempered Numa,[51] a bellicose Hostilio an upstanding and perennial Ancus Marcius.[52] The shrewd Priscus and the politician Servius were the first fruits of the Roman monarchy.[53]

Excellence and longevity surrounded the kings of Rome more than their emperors, because the former were sons of gallant youth and the latter of tired feuds and vendettas. The former conquered, the latter triumphed.

---

[51] Romulus was the legendary founder of Rome and Numa Pompilius his successor. They were the first and second of the seven kings who, according to Roman tradition, ruled Rome before the founding of the republic in 509 BC.

[52] Hostilio was the legendary third king of Rome and was succeeded by Ancus Marcius, who ruled Rome for 25 years.

[53] Lucius Tarquinius Priscus and Servius Tullius, were the fifth and sixth kings of Rome.

Longevity should be the primary concern of the Perfect King, since, typically, care and courage flourish in the beginning, then confidence enters, quickly followed by pride, then laziness, and, finally, the delights of hedonism, which finish everything off.

Of supreme importance is having an illustrious predecessor and patriarch whose example a future king can follow. The enlightened Frankish kings succeeded each other in their flourishing monarchy, with great efforts full of all virtue, but only because they followed the distinguished example set by King Clovis. But experience serves us faithfully, and history bears witness to the disasters that are born when a monarch lacks a strong masculine example to emulate. King Chlothar I ruined himself chasing the fame of his older brother King Childebert; Charles the Simple was captured by Herbert II, Count of Vermandois, and died a prisoner; and Charles the Inept was disposed of by his own nephew, the Roman Emperor Arnulf of Carinthia. The latter are but a few examples of the long list of kings turned tragedies, who lacked the wisdom that only an eminent patriarch can provide.

That warmth of a capable patriarch forms the foundation of an empire that, with the favor of Heaven, will last for some time; a father's radical substance of power, prudence, and courage remains in those children whom he carefully instructs; who could stop the impetus with which the Ottoman Empire started, growing from Ottoman, its first patriarch, to the Magnificent Suleiman? But it already began to decline under Selim II, who was confronted by a Holy Pontiff and resisted by a Catholic King. His empire only grew with discord as the Christian Kings threatened war, and if a brief Holy League could face it victorious, how much easier would it be to finish it fallen?[54]

Providence is the supreme author of empires, not blind and sometimes vulgar fortune. God forms them and undoes them, raises them up, and humbles them for his secret and highest ends; the faithful he raises to be the center of his glory and the unfaithful he humbles as an example of his punishment, and both serve as an illustration of the prodigious harmony that exists between his wisdom and power.[55]

It is always a great advantage to be a successor to a great and flourishing crown, as was the case with Xerxes and Dagobert,[56] who perfectly wielded power and excellence.

Divine Providence only declares itself for the most Christian kingdoms, having provided Hugh Capet[57] the ability to restore the monarchy for many centuries, continuing his lineage in so many famous kings and saints. And we cannot forget the great emulator of the divine, the Catholic Louis XIII,[58] the great restorer of Gaul, who banished from

---

54 A reference to the Battle of Lepanto, where the Holy Pontiff, Pope Pius V, and the Empire of Spain, under King Philip II, inflicted a major defeat on the Ottoman Empire. Here, Gracián laments the fact that the Christian Holy League chose not to capitalize on the victory, completely defeat the Ottoman Empire, and reconquer Constantinople.

55 A master of theology, Gracián is undoubtedly referencing St. Paul in Ephesians 1:11, where he states that God determines all things according to the counsel of his will.

56 Xerxes succeeded Darius the Great and Dagobert I succeeded Chlothar II.

57 Hugh Capet is the founder of the Capetian dynasty. It is among the largest and oldest royal houses in Europe, ruling without interruption from 987 to 1792.

58 King Louis XIII, also known as Louis the Just, was King of France in the early 17th century. Under his rule, France became a preeminent European power.

France all heresy and resolved to drive away all infidelity in the world.⁵⁹

Conversely, it is an extreme disadvantage for a prince to inherit a monarchy already despondent, courage fallen, idleness validated, virtue banished, vice enthroned, strength strained, reputation failed, happiness altered, and, having aged under the weight of darkness, like an old house, threatening to fall into total ruin at any moment.

A monarchy awaits the greatness of a Vespasian and of a Claudius II to restore it; it awaits the courage of a King Pepin, who drove out the heretics from France, and of a Hugh Capet to renew it; great thrones elevate great men; but to lesser men, the dwarfs, they are stumbling blocks that bring them down. Sadly, the latter is what usually happens, and the new king begins to suffer the same ailments as the monarchy he now commands.

Iniquity causes sickness to infect the healthy more often than virtue tends to cure the sick.⁶⁰ This was the miserable state of Spain when the unfortunate Rodrigo, prince of tarnished virtues, entered to reign in it. He entered the kingdom in a gulf of vices, finishing the old Gothic values of the great patriarchs who came before him: of Alaric, Athaulf, Sisebut, Reccared, Suintila, and Wamba. Everything was

---

59 A reference to the Siege of La Rochelle, which marked the height of the struggle between the Catholics and the Protestants in France and ended with a complete victory for King Louis.

60 Here, Gracián equates sickness with sin and states that due to man's wickedness (iniquity), it is much easier for a man to fall into vice than it is for virtue to cure him of his vice. He offers a remedy for this in the following paragraph. Well read and a master of philosophy, Gracián draws this wisdom from the *Epistulae Morales ad Lucilium*, also known as *The Moral Letters from a Stoic,* by Seneca. In one of the letters, Seneca states that "As we would avoid a person with a contagious illness, we should avoid people with bad habits and vice, both of which are highly infectious."

ruined, even the material defenses; his ineptitude and disgrace perhaps only undermined by the clumsiness and slovenliness of King Wittiza. The force of hedonism is great, and the violence of vice is even greater. And although a king may be generous and heroic by nature, vice will eventually have its way with him until there is nothing left of him.

And so the dependence of a king should be rooted in all that is Christian, so that he is sustained by the divine, and so that he will be capable and magnificent, constantly advancing his kingdom towards all that is virtuous, which is contrary to most other monarchies, which tend to dilapidate and go from order to disorder and from bad to worse. When virtue grows within a prince and becomes his new disposition, Heaven ensures itself to him, so that his last will be his best and his ending will be greater than his beginning. Nowhere is this more exemplified than in the life of King Fernando.

Governing also very much requires that the Perfect King come out to dwell among the people of the nation he rules over and minister to them all virtue. Either the people will ruin their king or their king will enrich them and win them for himself. The former is a matter of chance, and the latter is a matter of determination. The Assyrians attached their effeminate inclinations to their kings, even to their last one, Sardanapalus,[61] and to at least eight of his predecessors; monsters are what they deserve to be called. But the Lacedemonians, temperate and prudent, by their demeanor and commitment, inclined their heroic kings to every kind of virtue. While the Persians, inclined to every kind of vice and excessive expenditure on food, clothing, and

---
61 Sardanapalus, King of Assyria, lived in the 7th century BC. He was a decadent figure who spent his life in self-indulgence and died in an orgy of destruction. He exceeded all previous rulers in sloth and luxury, dressing in women's clothes, wearing makeup, and staffing many concubines, female and male. He also wrote his own epitaph, which stated that physical gratification was the only purpose of life.

materialism, so enraptured their kings that all of Asia was not enough to satiate their useless and vain extravagance. On the other hand, the Macedonians, a frugal and measured people, produced such extraordinary monarchs who, while they may have lacked pomp and ostentation, had an overabundance of greatness of spirit.

Ideally, a people will mirror the virtues and goodness of their king. This is what makes some kings exceptional and other kings common. The people should be a reflection of their king, and the king should be a tutor and father to his people. A nation is, in the end, to serve as the proper office for its heroic leader.

Fernando had great virtues as a man and especially as a king. Those who undertake to describe what a perfect monarch should be will tell you that virtues are easy to avoid but very difficult to attain.

Some have great virtues as men but do not have the disposition to rule as kings. Gratian[62] was very religious, but he was better suited for a monastery than for the imperial chair. Likewise, the Aragonese Ramiro[63] and the Portuguese Henrique[64] made for better clergymen than monarchs. And on the contrary, others possessed the great virtues that are required of a king but also a tremendous weakness for the vices that overcome man; in Alexander and Emperor Julius Caesar, we see these competing extremes. And in El Gran

---

62 Amiable and modest, Gratian was emperor of Rome. Generous, kind-hearted, chaste, and temperate, he was mindful of religious conduct, zealous for the Christian faith, and more concerned with the ecclesiastical policy of Rome than with its government and military affairs; hence, Gracián states, "he was better suited for a monastery than for the imperial chair."
63 King Ramiro II of Aragón abdicated his throne to become a monk.
64 King Henrique was both a Cardinal in the Catholic Church and King of Portugal.

Batallador, The Great Battler, Don Jaime I,[65] we see some of the carelessness that afflicts a man[66] but the greatness of a ruler too; at the age of ten, he wielded the scepter and ascended to the throne of Aragón with the courage of thirty and the maturity of a hundred.

The royal elements of kingship are sublime and of superior command and authority. They are capable of filling great voids in ordinary men and turning them into competent rulers, as in the example of King Don Denis of Portugal[67] and King Henry IV of France, who, for all his faults as a man, will always be celebrated because he was distinguished as a king; and in great men, they move to create even greater rulers, like King Alfonso the Magnanimous,[68] who possessed all the virtues of both an exceptional man and a remarkable king; to him we look when we seek preeminence to esteem and emulate, in both our private and public life.

What does it matter if one is a great mathematician but not even a substandard leader? The fabric of the universe

---

65 King Jaime I, also known as Jaime the Conqueror, is the greatest and most renowned of the medieval kings of Aragón, whose early life served as a hard school for the forging of his character. Fearless even as a youth, he once fought an Aragonese noble in hand-to-hand combat, took part in the siege of Castejón, and successfully waged the second war of reconquest in the Kingdom of Valencia. He once recounted being wounded in battle in his autobiography, *Llibre dels fets (Book of Deeds)*: "I removed the arrow, and blood came out, rushing down my face. I wiped it off with a cloth and went away laughing, because I did not want my soldiers to be alarmed or lose confidence." In 1856, King Jamie's mummified body was exhumed when the monastery he was buried in underwent repair. A photograph that was taken of the king's face showed the wound above his left eyebrow that he mentioned in his book.

66 A reference to King Jaime's many extramarital affairs.

67 King Denis of Portugal who is considered the *Pai da Pátria* (the father of his country) by the historian Duarte Nunes de Leão.

68 King Alfonso V of Aragón is considered the most brilliant of 15th century monarchs; respected by both friend and foe, he was given the title of "the Magnanimous" by his contemporaries.

cannot be corrected if you are on the verge of losing your kingdom.[69]

These royal virtues, which are jewels capable of creating greatness, are dependent on the measure of a man; in mediocre men, they accomplish nothing, but in superlative men, like the great Goth, King Wamba,[70] they make the man extraordinary. Mediocre men are ignorant, but superlative men are brave.[71]

However, the perfection of a king—of an Emperor Otto, a King Clovis, or a King Fernando III of Castilla—is limited and not without Providence, requiring him to follow the example set by the divine. Wise nature has deposited all the faculties needed for life in the head.[72]

These jewels separated the great emperor, King Rudolf I, from his compeers and made him the first King of Germany.

----

[69] The interpretive meaning is that it does not matter how great a man is if he is incapable of leading others, particularly those closest to him. Lack of leadership renders a man impotent, ineffectual, and unable to correct the wrongs around him.

[70] King Wamba was a farmer who was elected King of Spain. As king, he subdued a separatist rebellion in Gaul (France) and other territories in his realm, personally leading his armies across the Pyrenees, defeating the rebel forces, and escorting them back to Toledo as captives. A gracious king, he once met an ambitious noble named Paul in battle who thought he could easily dispose of the much older Wamba and claim his throne. When the king destroyed his army and took him prisoner, Paul expected to be found guilty of treason and decapitated, but King Wamba simply ordered that his hair be shaved off. Wamba lived the final seven years of his life as a monk.

[71] "Mediocre men are ignorant, but superlative men are brave." Gracián implies that mediocre men are too ignorant to know when Providence is trying to make them great through hardship and struggle, the two crucibles that produce virtue. Superior men are brave and lean into the challenges presented to them, while mediocre men, too ignorant to see them as opportunities, run from them.

[72] A reference to Romans 7:25, where St. Paul wrote, "It is with the mind that we serve God."

They serve as a Christian foundation and as evidence, so that a king may be counted among the perfect ones, lest he be seen as politically impious and condemned as blind and dumb.

The best of the nonbelievers was the Emperor Trajan,[73] who was so great that even the Catholics envied him, and many Fathers of the Church prayed for him, with great affection, so that he may be redeemed from any eternal unhappiness.[74] But how does he compare to the Christian, the Emperor Theodosius? Trajan equals him in the excellence of virtues, but Theodosius exceeds him in the plurality of them. Trajan requested honor, and Theodosius requested merit; one sought respect, and the other sought excellence. Trajan wanted to be triumphant over his enemies, while Theodosius wanted to be victorious over life; he was greater than Trajan in the temperance of both the mind and body.

Henry IV and Louis IX, both of France, were consummated among emperors and kings, proof that what is holy will always best what is secular.[75]

Impiety leads to unhappiness, which opposes itself to personal victory and self-improvement; in this way, many kings have victimized themselves and amounted to nothing. One of them was Emperor Claudius, of whom the philosophical

---

73 **Emperor Trajan is considered one of the Five Good Emperors of Rome. He was a philanthropic ruler and a successful soldier-emperor who led the Roman Empire to its greatest territorial extent by the time of his death. He was given the title of *optimus* (the best) by the Roman Senate.**

74 **Trajan did not seek out Christians to persecute, and so Gracián says that because of this and his philanthropy as a ruler, the Catholics prayed for him in hopes that he would be spared from eternal damnation.**

75 **King Henry IV of France and King Louis IX of France were both pious rulers. Gracián credits their faith in Christianity for their success.**

Seneca said, "No one knew that he had ceased to be, because no one knew that he had begun to be." While Charles the Inept lived in France he might as well have been dead, and Murad[76] and Muhammad, who could easily have been children of something, even of greatness, fixed their happiness on nothing.

But impious men are tolerable extremes, since there exist greater monstrosities—men that fill their void of virtues with abominable vices and destroy everything. Emperor Nero was an egregious wonder, amphibious between man and beast; the first six years he competed with the best kings, and the last six with the worst.[77] Heaven sent an oracle of prudence to be a teacher to this monster of wickedness, but teachings are of little use when a man is naturally repugnant. Imagine how much worse he would have been had he not had the great philosopher![78]

Elagabalus[79] lives in infamy; he degenerated even though he was already a brute, and his very memory is an affront to wise nature. Both he and Nero had abominable vices as men and kings; they sinned on both hands.

The mistakes of kings are eternal, and they are commonly born in the most hidden parts of their palaces and then fly to the public square. They error in an instant and it is

---

76   Murad III was sultan of the Ottoman Empire. He began his reign by having his five younger brothers strangled.
77   Emperor Nero is remembered as a monster and sadist with a chilling list of crimes to his name, from burning down his own capital city to sleeping with his mother and murdering many of his close relatives.
78   A reference to Seneca, the stoic philosopher who was appointed tutor to the young Nero. Later in life, Nero would order him to commit suicide in front of his wife.
79   Elagabalus became Emperor of Rome at age seventeen and his short reign was notorious for sex scandals and religious controversy.

forever, and their momentary inadvertence is condemned to become perennial news.

Very little must be lacking to be an imperfect entity, and yet everything must be in surplus for there to be perfection, especially when we are speaking of the most important category among the order of things, which is that of king.

-IV-
A King of Virtue

The virtues or vices of a king are always very visible and therefore more noticeable. Errors bar excellence and easily indict, because those under obligation remain the least hidden from scrutiny.

Foreign courts gossiped about some slight ailments in Fernando, seemingly very interested in them, as if they were Fernando's natural disposition, but those slights were excusable because he prevailed over them and they yielded to him. If he failed, it was not because they overcame him, but because he was overtaken by the effects of momentary occasions and not vice; eventually, time diminished them.[80] It is a contradiction that foreign courts attribute everything bad to him and Spaniards deny him everything good; the former pile up the blame, and the latter seize the successes.

It is normal for people to note some faults, but what is important is that they do not note excesses. The truth is that what may seem extreme to one person is nothing more

---

80 Gracián paints a picture of King Fernando as a man who is aware of his shortcomings, who is at war with them, and who, over time, defeats them. He also seems to be of the opinion that the vices of a man matter more when he yields to them, and they matter less when they yield to him. A student of stoicism, his opinion is influenced by Seneca, who said, "A wise man finds the evils within himself and goes to war with them."

than perfect balance to another. Fernando tempered with his moderation the prodigality of two of his predecessor kings, and if he was restrained with others, much more so with himself: with his velvet sleeve and the satin doublet of his Catholic Queen Isabella, he ruled with plausibility. He did not want to retract his mercies nor did he want his successors to retract them.

The Perfect King must be universal in talent and singular in governing. He must be a great leader, a great counselor to himself, a great judge, a great economist, and even a great religious dignitary, but, most of all, he must be a maximum king.

Some do not consider a king great unless he is a great military leader and a great fighter, but this narrows the role of a monarch to that of a captain and confuses that which is superior with that which is inferior. Royal eminence is not in fighting but in governing. This ought to be the pledge of a great king who, although he may be universal in eminence, of maximum judgment, of relevant wit, and of heroic courage, goes to extremes to govern well, even at times violating himself as if he were stealing from his natural bellicose inclination, judging the apex of each situation with the royal virtues and coat of arms of a proper and poised king.

Emperor Aurelian was an excellent captain, but not an excellent emperor. Charles of Burgundy may have been an illustrious fighter, but he was not an illustrious ruler. The tyrant Saturninus[81] knew himself when they put the crown

---

81 Lucius Antonius Saturninus was a Roman general who was made governor of Rome's northern territories, what is now Switzerland and parts of Germany. He led a rebellion known as the Revolt of Saturninus, where he was defeated by the future emperor, General Trajan. Very little is known of him since he was subject to *damnatio memoriae,* "condemnation of memory," following his defeat and death: Rome destroyed all official records of him, thus excluding him from history.

on him: "Today, I say, comrades, you have lost a good general and created a bad governor." Heroic promises in both the military and government are plausible for a king but not probable. Yes, the Christian Don Jaime and the Turkish Mahomet achieved the immortal reputations of being both great warriors and rulers, but, when well examined and due to political rigor, the office of king is not to be a captain. The duty is too universal, too comprehensive; it embraces too much importance. Of a consummate king, of a perfect prince, of a Trajan, of a Charlemagne, of a Don Fernando the Catholic, a hundred famous men could be made if their attributes were to be distributed, if their virtues were to be divided.

All the jobs that the great Roman Republic distributed among so many great men—governors, generals, consuls, dictators, tribunes, censors, and mentors—were united around only one Caesar, who needed to be a Perfect King, by obligation and with eminence.

One should never dedicate everything to a single responsibility, which would be to steal attention from others of equal importance. By luck, the great Louis of France[82] did not get carried away with his bellicosity and lose sight of justice, religion, government, economy, and his other royal obligations.

While at war, Charlemagne attended to the peace, the increase, and the happiness of his kingdom. While fighting

---

82 Louis IX of France, also known as Louis the Saint, is remembered for his many crusades against the enemies of Christianity as well as for his reforms to the French legal system and his promotion of Catholicism and the arts. His kingdom was considered the greatest in Europe, both politically and economically, and he was regarded as *primus inter pares,* "first among equals," by the kings of Europe. He commanded the largest army and ruled the largest and wealthiest kingdom. During his reign, his court was the center of European art and intellectual thought.

in Germania, he instituted the famous University of Paris and the great Parliament of France.

But most kings who are warriors at heart destroy their kingdoms more than their opponents; trying to vanquish their enemies, they make war on themselves, impoverishing their states of gold and people, which are the greatest and principal wealth.

In this, Fernando was very shrewd, for he filled Spain with triumphs and riches. Fighting in one kingdom, he triumphed in the others. He enriched Spain temporally and spiritually. He advanced the militia and justice, the former with armies, the latter with courts.

He always ruled according to the occasion, the maximum aphorism of his politics. To correspond the genius of a prince with the current state of the monarchy is luck; to be violated and forced to mitigate is prudence. The former has the advantage of being connatural and ensures duration with ease; the latter deserves the glory of diligence and application.

It is necessary for a king to adjust his inclinations to the disposition of the monarchy, either by nature or by ingenuity.

At one moment, a sovereign warrior might be needed, in another, a peaceful king; unhappiness lies in inflexibility when meeting contingencies. The Franks had a tranquil Childeric when a Mars[83] was needed, and, conversely, a bellicose Francis when his kingdom and all Christendom needed peace to flourish.[84]

---

83 Mars is the Roman god of war.

84 Gracián mentions two kings whose natural dispositions did not match the needs of their kingdoms but who adjusted their inclinations to meet the occasions. King Childeric I went to war to cement his kingdom after the fall of the western Roman Empire, and King Francis I signed the Peace of Cateau-Cambrésis to end the Italian wars after sixty-five years; both kings rose to occasions that were contradictory to their natural predisposition.

Many kings would have been sons of fame if they had first been sons of season and occasion: which speaks to my point about the importance of actions, especially royal actions. Ruling requires perfection from a king at all times, in all thoughts, words, and deeds.

The Portuguese King Sebastian came into the monarchy with certainty, but he could not find moderation for his overriding ambitions nor a natural place to rest his generous spirit; what he violently sought, a few centuries earlier, he could have attained. He would have been another Caesar and Lisbon another Rome. So lamentable! He was a king truly worthy of a better time![85]

This is the foundation of greatness: growing in strength, adjusting to the current state and its different seasons, in emulation of the great kings who precede and in continued courage, without much difference between them or variation of scepters, so that consistent fortune will declare her favor, neither changing nor weakening the accredited military and political value of a king and his kingdom.

So that when arms are demanded because of increased tensions and the temptation of fame and military bravery is in its fervor, favorable fortune will help a prudent and tempered king succeed, by rewarding his poise with cooling circumstances and victory.

---

85 A reference to the death of the young King Sebastian in the Battle of Alcácer Quibir. Unable to find moderation for his religious zeal, he reversed the policy of his grandfather, Don Juan III, of avoiding costly religious conquests. Against the advice of his uncle, King Philip II, and his own commanders, Sebastian sailed to Morocco and marched into battle against the Muslim king, Abd Al-Malik, who led more than 60,000 soldiers. Sebastian was killed in battle, the Portuguese army was decimated, and Portugal was left without a king. Gracián also references parts of this story in his fourth book, *El Discreto: The Complete Man (1646)*, to stress the importance of patience.

The Aragonese and the Castillians shook off the shameful African yoke with such alacrity; and with the continued courage of their famous kings, they were able to help their neighbors and even finish driving out the Moors from most of Spain. The value and capacity of these kings was not only enough to fill their states, but more than enough to fill the whole world.[86]

King Don Sancho died the death of heroes, in the tightest of straits, intent on retaking the City of Huesca from the Moors, the key to his kingdoms, the gateway to his Christian conquests, and awaiting help from an army of kings.[87] But he was succeeded by the undefeated King Don Pedro,[88] his son and prince of occasion, who not only made up for but also improved the loss of his father.[89] He wielded the sword instead of the scepter, thirsty for unfaithful blood, and avenged the fatal paternal arrow that struck his father.

All empires have their increases, but their capacity to increase is only in accordance with the value of their king; it can

---

86 A reference to King Jaime I of Aragón and King Fernando III of Castilla, who helped various kingdoms in Spain drive out the Moors. These great Christian kings of the north were relentless in their crusades to rid Spain of the Islamic invaders, who, for centuries, had been subjecting European Christian men to death and taking the women and children as slaves.

87 In 1094, King Sancho Ramirez was struck and killed by an arrow in the Battle of Alcoraz during the siege on the City of Huesca.

88 King Pedro I was the eldest son of Sancho Ramírez, from whom he inherited the crown of Aragón. He continued his father's close alliance with the Catholic Church and pursued his military thrust south against the invading Moors with great success. Don Pedro is considered to have been an expert in war.

89 When King Sancho was killed during the siege of Huesca, a strategic Muslim city, his son King Pedro renewed the offensive and, at nearby Alcoraz, met a large Muslim army led by Al-Mustain, whom he completely destroyed. The besieged city surrendered to the valiant Aragonese King nine days later.

conserve itself with a king of average value, which is enough not to decline; however, more kingdoms have perished for lack of value than for excess.

There exist kingdoms that ask for a warlike king, like bellicose France. Others, on the contrary, are pacifist, like England, although by accident or convenience, this may sometimes vary.

Some need a king inclined to justice and others to clemency, and after one extreme is experienced, the other is usually well received in the same republic. The prodigal kings Juan II of Aragón and Enrique of Castilla were succeeded by a prudent guardian, Fernando,[90] who twice redeemed the crown, first from his own vassals and then from his enemies.[91] In Portugal, the benignity of King Don Manuel I was well embraced after the rigors of his predecessor, Don Juan. It is with alternation and a variety of influences that empires are better preserved.

When neighboring kings are martial and bellicose, a king fattened by entertainment and the delights of peace is fatal, dangerous, and even despised. His laxity increases pride in his opponents, despair in his vassals and, if another king is coveted, serious unhappiness in his kingdom.

It is not politics, but sagacity and knowledge that make up for a lack of military expertise. This is how Louis of France

---

90 Unlike the kings whom Fernando succeeded, who were wasteful and had extravagant spending habits, Fernando was prudent and measured with the kingdom's finances.

91 "First from his own vassals and then from his enemies." The former is a reference to the crown of Aragón, which he inherited, and the latter is a reference to the crown of Castilla, which he won after emerging victorious during the War of the Castilian Succession.

competed with the brave warrior Charles of Burgundy, showing how much greater skill is than force.⁹²

Fernando was accompanied by contemporaries of his same genius: they were shrewd, attentive, and political. It was an era of men who were kings; yet other eras belong to men who are more warriors than kings; they compete with each other in courage, emulating each other's fame. This holds true with the victorious Charles V in Spain, the bellicose Francis I in France, and the magnificent Suleiman in Turkey, all three great warriors. Each of them would have taken over the whole world if they were not each other's antagonists, each one breaking the other's power and confronting one another in their efforts.

At other times, the kings are all just, pious, religious, and sons of the Exalted One. Emperor Henry in Germany, Robert in France, Canute in England, and Boleslaw in Poland.⁹³

And yet other kings only exist to delight in the pleasures of life and, consequently, are remiss and negligent. Kings can awaken or cause slumber in each other, and, like domesticated birds, they can provoke each other to song or silence. Even in cruelty, they compete, and even in different eras, just as the three Pedros in Spain erred.⁹⁴

----

92 Louis XI was not a skilled warrior like Charles the Bold of Burgundy, but he was a wise and superior diplomat. Rather than face the Burgandian warrior alone, he negotiated alliances between France, Switzerland, and Austria. Shortly afterwards, the Swiss Confederacy declared war on Burgundy and utterly defeated its army, killing Charles the Bold in the Battle of Nancy.

93 A reference to Henry III (the Pious), Robert I (the Wise), Canute I (the Great), and Boleslaw I (the Brave), who were all pious rulers and each other's contemporaries.

94 A reference to King Pedro the Cruel of Castilla, King Pedro II of Aragón, who allied himself with the heretics and abandoned his son Jaime, and the bellicose King Pedro IV of Aragón.

Like the Catholic Fernando, the Perfect King must combine the diplomacy of King Louis XI, the prudence of Roman Emperor Maximilian I, the wisdom of Pope Alexander VI, and the astuteness of Ludovico Sforza, so that if he were to challenge each one of them in their realm of mastery, he would win.

It was an era of politicians and Fernando the professor of Prima.[95] Specifically, he was a prudent politician more than an astute politician, which is a big difference.[96]

It is a vulgar affront to wisdom to confuse it with cunning: some consider as wise only the deceitful and even wiser the one who knows how to best pretend, dissimulate, and defraud, not realizing that the punishment of such behavior is always to perish in deceit. The statesmen venerate two idols, the two oracles of politics: Tiberius and Louis XI. They praise their dissimulation and they exaggerate their cunning; but I attribute this reputation more to the commentary of the two writers, who were Tacitus[97] and Comines,[98] than to the accuracy of their deeds.

I have always considered political trickery and speeches useless and a gateway to despondency, since they have brought many kings to the point of losing their crowns. What they couldn't achieve through riches, they tried to achieve through affectation, and what they should have attempted

---

95   Prima is Latin for "The First."

96   **Prudent implies sagacity in adapting a means to an end. It is circumspect in action and in determining any line of conduct, careful, discreet, and sensible as opposed to rash, while astute is quickly and critically discerning.**

97   **Publius Cornelius Tacitus, known simply as Tacitus, was a Roman historian and politician. He is widely regarded as one of the greatest Roman historians by modern scholars.**

98   **Philippe de Commines was a writer and diplomat in the courts of Burgundy and France. He is considered the first modern writer and the first critical and philosophical historian of modern times.**

to achieve for the love of virtue, they attempted in order to conceal the horror of their cruelties.

Because of this, many reached the extreme of despair, enveloped in affectation, and condemned to banishment. To die in life and continue living is an intolerable death; it is an advantage to have a Caligula and a Nero die and remain dead so as not to afflict humanity with more atrocities; but it is an insufferable burden for a living king to see his authority die, yet continue to live and experience contempt.

It is not enough to hear and see the one from whom the effects emanate. Good speeches can only be validated through works. Politics and orations that are resolved in fantastic subtleties and affected by artifice are useless, and the kings who beget them are rulers of much chimera and of no benefit.

How much better a politician was Louis the Ninth than the Eleventh, both Frenchmen, without so much metaphysics or political machine! The Holy King brought out the natural war of France and cast it upon the enemies of the Lord;[99] he brought war to the infidels, but his successors brought it back, and Christianity never again went out to challenge them, either in Europe or from any other Christian confine, producing little in fruit and even less in happiness. Had they continued, the name of Mohammed would have already been forgotten in all of Europe, Africa, and Asia. Oh, a point worthy of observation and also of lamentation! That today we see Christianity burning in wars against itself while all paganism is resting! The Christians are bathed in blood and the Infidels in roses!

---
99 A reference to King Louis IX, also known as Saint Louis, and his crusades against Islam. Specifically the seventh crusade, the eighth crusade, and his four years spent strengthening the Kingdom of Jerusalem.

Honest and masterful was Fernando's governing, sure and firm, and not wrapped in illusions and chimera. Useful, because it yielded him kingdoms his entire life. Honest, because it made him deserving of the Catholic coat of arms. He conquered kingdoms for Christ, crowns as thrones of his Cross, provinces for his fields of the Faith, and, in the end, he was able to unite earth with Heaven.

The Perfect King is a master of virtue and occasions, the latter of which cuts to measure the former. Some kings have excellent talents, but they lack the opportunities to use them. And on the contrary, others have the opportunities and lack the talents; I do not know which one I condemn for greater unhappiness.

He does not affect occasions, nor does he violate them; on the contrary, his wisdom invites him to go with them. Only the less capable go hunting for opportunities, taking the universe out of its perfect balance and, in the end, becoming oppressed by their own infirmity.

-V-
A King of Capable Capacity

It is the greatest asset and the sunshine of others, prodigious capacity, the sure foundation of royal greatness.

"The world will be happy," said Plato, "when wise kings begin to reign or those reigning begin to be wise." The constitutive royal primary of the Perfect King is having a great capacity, because a king of much capacity is a king of much substance; he is the head of his kingdom's understanding; therefore, his greatest attribute must be a large capacity to comprehend, grasp, perceive, discern, and understand.

Capacity constitutes men; incapacity, monsters. The former constitutes a Caesar[100] who establishes a monarchy; the latter, a Gallienus[101] who loses it; the former encourages Cyrus[102] to glorious achievements; the latter, a Darius[103]

---

[100] Gaius Julius Caesar, who, as governor of Gaul, marched on Rome, defeated the Roman army under General Pompey, and became the absolute ruler of the Roman Empire.

[101] Publius Licinius Egnatius Gallienus was Roman emperor during the Crisis of the Third Century, which nearly caused the collapse of the empire.

[102] Cyrus the Great, widely considered by scholars to be one of history's greatest rulers.

[103] Darius the Great is considered a great leader by most scholars but not by Gracián, who condemns him for being driven more towards leisure than towards achievements.

to leisure and rest; and so from capacity sprouts virtue in Pelayo;[104] from incapacity, sinister proclivities in Rodrigo;[105] one births exploits in Romulus,[106] and the other abominations, as seen in Rome's last king, Lucius Tarquinius.[107]

All the great kings, eternalized in the archives of fame and in the immortal catalogs of applause, possessed this principle of wealth, without which there can be no greatness.

It is innate, not acquired, the optimal gift, the perfect gift, which descends from the Father of Enlightenment. It is a good that grows with diligence and is perfected with experience.

It is the foundation of life and politics, and of that great art of being a great king, but it can only be found in great trials: Jaime I of Aragón, Louis XI of France, Matthias Corvinus of Hungary, Emperor Maximilian, Stephen Báthory of Poland, and Fernando of Spain serve as qualified proof.[108]

Capacity is the underpinning of prudence, without which neither years of work nor diligence can ever create a master. With it, the young men are old, and without it, the old men are young men.[109] Otto III deserves the superlative of

---

104 Pelayo was the founder of the Christian Kingdom of Asturias in northern Spain.

105 Rodrigo was the last king of the Visigoths and here, Gracián mentions his rape of a young girl who was the daughter of the governor of Ceuta as "sinister proclivities."

106 Romulus was the legendary founder and first king of Rome.

107 Lucius Tarquinius Superbus, the last king of Rome. He was overthrown and sent into exile.

108 Here, Gracián gives a list of monarchs who were perfected by their trials and whose capacity, according to him, grew exponentially because of them.

109 "With it, the young men are old, and without it, the old men are young men." With prudence, young men have the wisdom of a sage, but without it, old men have the folly of youth.

esteem; I say it is right that he should be called the "Miracle of the World," because at the age of eleven, he was made emperor and performed his duties well; his lack of gray hair is made up for by his successes, and everyone admired his century of maturity in only two decades of age.[110]

But where extremities of great capacity were found was in Queen Semiramis,[111] the one who founded Babylon and commanded Asia: forty years she prevailed in faith in an art dominated by men. She insisted on ruling as her late husband did, and with womanly application she put down the ailments of her kingdom; no costume would ever be enough to disguise her sex if capacity did not prove her abilities.

Capacity is the other pillar, which, side by side with courage, ensures both reputation and, in competition, renewed victory. Charles V[112] was not called wise because of his studies or sciences but because he knew how to govern, which is the proof of true knowledge in kings; without putting on the harness, he recovered all of France and almost all the foreign lands his predecessors had lost, and, without forsaking the royal throne, he rejected back to Britannia the English.

---

110 Otto III had a considerably high intellect and was very advanced for his age. He spoke three languages, was well versed in both Greek and Roman culture, and his contemporaries called him *mirabilia mundi*, the "Miracle of the World."

111 Semiramis ruled the Neo-Assyrian Empire. Setting out to emulate the agenda of her late husband, she ordered Babylon to be built on the banks of the Euphrates, conquered much of the Middle East, and stabilized the empire after a civil war.

112 King Charles V of France, also called Charles the Wise. His reign marked an early high point for France during the Hundred Years' War, with his armies recovering much of the territory held by the English and successfully reversing the military losses of his predecessors.

But for these levels of greatness, it is necessary to have the intelligence of a Justinian,[113] the politics of a Louis,[114] and the prudence of Philip II.[115] To be a Gallienus and equal them in knowledge but exceed them in ineffectiveness is to want to keep the palace but not the empire.[116]

Through hardship, knowledge and courage are acquired; only then can Heaven amplify capacity and a Perfect King be made: a Moses, to be legislator and leader of the Republic of God. A brave David, to be jealous, wise, and to celebrate the honor of the Most High. A Caesar, to blazon the pen and the sword. An Agesilaus II, whose words deserved to be the first in the book of the discreet, and his deeds in the book of the brave.[117] A Constantine the Great, authorizing the councils and leading the armies. A Justinian, giving arms and laws to the Empire. An Alfonso the Magnanimous, superior in both administration and military campaigns. A Shah Ismail, whose legacy as a sage is the stamp of his victorious sword.[118] A Francis I of France, surrounded by sages and warlords. A Philip II of Spain, who began brave and ended prudent.

Capacity is an invaluable jewel that requires the following eminent faculties: promptness in intelligence and maturity

---

113   A reference to Justinian I, Emperor of the Eastern Roman Empire.
114   A reference to Louis XI of France, known for his political acumen.
115   Philip II of Spain, also known as Philip the Prudent.
116   "Keep the palace but not the empire" is a reference to Gallienus' numerous military victories against usurpers and Germanic tribes and his inability to prevent the secession of important provinces.
117   A reference to the chronicled history of Agesilaus and the Kingdom of Sparta by the Greek historian Xenophon of Athens.
118   Ismail's greatest legacy was establishing an empire that lasted over 200 years.

in judgment; understanding precedes resolution, and intelligence is the dawn of prudence.

An understanding king, a Casimir of Poland,[119] I say, is all of these points in one. He first mastered himself, so that later he would be master of all through the power of experience. Augustus[120] first envisioned his whole empire in his head, and then he held it in his fist. He opened and closed at will the Gates of Janus, which was the same as having in his hand the keys of the Universe, lord of war and peace.[121]

The authority and reputation of the African, Jacob Almanzor,[122] was everywhere, because these cognitive requirements were all in him.

A prudent king, whose great judgment is the contrast of all great wealth, weighs talents, measures funds, appreciates eminence, examines merits, and judiciously raises ministers and captains who deserve to be emperors, and much more. Like Antoninus,[123] he distributes his duties, not for ease of his mind, but by the examination of his rigorous judgment.

---

119   Casimir III, also known as Casimir the Great, inherited a kingdom weakened by war and made it prosperous and wealthy. He reformed the Polish army, doubled the size of his kingdom, reformed the judicial system, and introduced legal codes.

120   Gaius Julius Caesar Augustus, the founder of the Roman Empire.

121   A reference to the Temple of Janus, which was a small temple with a statue of Janus, the two-faced god of boundaries and beginnings, inside. Its doors were known as the "Gates of Janus," which were closed in times of peace and opened in times of war.

122   Jacob Almanzor was a military leader and ruler in Islamic Iberia. At the height of his rule, he had seventy thousand European Christian slaves, many of them women.

123   Antoninus Pius was Emperor of the Roman Empire and is considered the fourth of the Five Good Emperors. An effective administrator, he left his successors a large surplus in the treasury, expanded free access to drinking water, encouraged legal conformity, and facilitated the enfranchisement of freed slaves.

A shrewd king, a royal *Argos*[124] who foresees everything. An emulator of Janus, the great King of Cyprus, capable of comprehending the incomprehensible. His own are wary of him, strangers fear him, and everyone attends to him, because he understands everyone.

A penetrating king, who discovers more with a single glance than others with eternal vigilance: to the one with much perception, nothing is missed; and to the one who penetrates everything, nothing is hidden. Henry IV of France had a transcendent intelligence, such that even his intentions commanded a healthy fear; he was a diviner of the greatest depth, making annotations of the spirit, of the natural, and of inclinations.

A heedful king, who sees all, hears all, smells all, and touches all. Vespasian's[125] ears were not sickened by the common royal ailments: the adulteries of truth, of sinister information, or the treacheries of flattery.

An attentive king, who neither sleeps nor lets sleep those who help him to be king: his subordinates. A lion when he watches, a lion when he sleeps, his eyes are always open, both to reality and false appearances. Oh, the attentiveness of the prudent Philip of Spain and his comparison of the loom with the throne, where a king is always attentive to every thread that breaks![126]

A sensitive king, may he be stung, and may the losses hurt him in the depths of his heart. Some have paradoxical

---

124 *Argos* in Spanish refers to a very vigilant person.

125 Vespian was Emperor of the Roman Empire. His fiscal reforms and consolidation of the empire generated political stability and a vast Roman building program. He was known for his wit and his amiable manner, along with his commanding personality and military prowess.

126 A loom is an instrument for making fabric by weaving yarn or thread.

reasoning and justify having a state of indolence and a magnanimity of insensitivity. But when sensitive nature formed its living creatures, it intended for sensitivity to be their only means of preservation, and so it wants its kings to be sensitive to their affairs.

Who will not abhor the stupidity of the Emperor Gallienus? When the bad news of the rebellious provinces and of the lost kingdoms, which were more than twenty in number, reached him, he very calmly replied, "Eh, we shall do well without the vegetables of Egypt! Why should we care for the hemp of France?" Oh, inept insensibility! That a king would see to it that the figs are green all year round, but not see to it that his empire flourishes! Oh, ignorant insensibility! That he seeks inventions to make the grapes last two and three years but suffers the loss of his kingdom. The world has no lack of these pernicious flatterers who canonize their magnanimity of barbarity and their constancy to stupidity; and most times, their audacity goes so far as to sell as great political subtlety what is an abhorrent negligence. A king must guard himself, because while he lives, he will be a hero to his flatterers and tolerated by others, but eventually, his deeds will be judged in the land of the living.

Magnanimous was the Emperor Augustus, whose name should ring the bell of our hearts. He felt so much the slaughter of the Roman legions in Germania that he struck the ground with his feet and the walls with his head; he tore his clothing and refused to cut his hair for months. Years afterward, he would still cry out, repeating: "What have you done with my legions, Quintilius Varus? Give me back my valiant soldiers!"[127] What account do we have of such

---

[127] A reference to the Battle of Teutoburg Forest, where, under Roman General Quintilius Varus, three Roman legions were ambushed and massacred. A Roman legion consisted of 6,000 men, so approximately 18,000 soldiers were killed: a very significant amount.

a strenuous captain? He was not seen to laugh for months nor eat for days. This is true authority and not contrary to majesty. Rodrigo never thought that his doom was so imminent; Rehoboam[128] never bothered to look closely at his possible ruin, while a lack of acumen costs Jean d'Albret[129] and Astiages[130] their crowns.

This understanding, prudent, shrewd, penetrating, lively, attentive, sensitive, and, in a word, wise, king, was the Catholic Fernando, a king of the greatest capacity, qualified with facts and exercised on so many occasions. His knowledge was useful, and, although he had more than enough courage, he governed with skill.

Fernando was not fortunate but prudent, for prudence is the mother of good fortune. Prudence frequently produces happiness, just as imprudence produces misfortune, and this is why all the most prudent kings have been very favored.

What good is the great wealth of a Don Juan II of Castilla if there is no wise application?[131] May an incapable king recognize his shortcomings, apply himself, and choose more precisely. Because to bury superior talent in idleness and vice is worthy of condemnation.

---

128 Rehoboam was King of Judah when it was invaded and defeated by King Shishak of Egypt.

129 A reference to King John III of Navarre, who, after several military and political defeats, became a recluse and died of depression in his castle. He was a Frenchman who became king of Navarre through marriage, and that seems to be the reason why Gracián refers to him in French.

130 Astyages was the last king of the Median Empire. He was dethroned by his grandson, Cyrus the Great.

131 A reference to King Juan II of Castilla and his lack of capacity as a ruler. He was known to spend his time verse-making, hunting, and holding tournaments, rather than governing.

In all of life, intermediate skill with application is better than rare talent without it. Confidence is the mother of carelessness, and this is the plague of great rulers. The death of a king birthed a new dawn and required Vespasian to die on his feet, rejecting temptation in order to devise a better way to live.[132] The remission of all vices in a king is a prerequisite to attaining superior temperament and victory. There were many great kings, not so much because of their great talents but because of their praiseworthy continuous self-perfection.

Great kings do not spare their office or themselves of the greatest recreations, penetrating the theater of wild beasts with the audience of their vassals. But they always reserve sight for entertainment and the ear for information.

It is bad to dream of being king when you do not have the capacity of a king; and worse, to be king when you do not want to be. The latter of these is an unconscionable reality.

Fernando competed against the requirements of Heaven and applied himself to compose a Perfect King, a maximum monarch: forty years he reigned, without wasting a single one, and he worked more than forty kings together. He is an earthly example worthy of emulation.

The crowned tree is a scepter that bears fruit as evidence of deeds. And if wise nature asks her to bear fruit every year, how much more does God demand this from his heroes? Yet a lush but barren fig tree, idly occupying a field, is like a useless king occupying the royal throne. He serves only as a hindrance to another who would crown the kingdom with the fertile branches of his arms.

---

132 A reference and contrast between the gluttonous Emperor Vitellius and the wise Emperor Vespasian, who spent money on public works and the restoration and beautification of Rome. He constructed the Temple of Peace, public baths, and the Colosseum. He also spent money on education and gave teachers royal treatment.

Hercules hung on the threshold of fame a new trophy every year—first the lion, then the hydra—he was an imagined hero in whom the ancients conceived a true king, always compelled to new and glorious endeavors.

The real Hercules was the Catholic Fernando; with more exploits than days, he gained a kingdom every year, acquiring Aragón by inheritance, Castilla by dowry, Granada by valor, India by wit, Naples by industry, Navarre by religion, and all by his great capacity.

The undertakings of a king are various, and all of them are heroic. They must all be embraced as Stephen I of Hungary[133] did: not by choice but by circumstance. Not like those suggested to Alexander the Great by his taste but those demanded by necessity of Alexander Severus.[134]

Thus, different circumstances will mean the showcasing of different capabilities. Not all will need to showcase the courage of Gustavus I of Sweden or King Alfonso the Magnanimous of Naples, but they may still gain a greater reputation than those of a military nature. Justinian deserved more glory for his laws than Aurelian[135] for his weapons. Fernando was more famous for having founded with integrity the caretaking of the Sacred Court of the Inquisition than for having established his monarchy. And he gained more by driving the Jews out of Spain than by having made Spain mistress of so many nations.

---

133 Stephen of Hungary, King and Saint, is considered one of the most important statesmen in the history of Hungary. He gave his kingdom almost 40 years of peace and stability.

134 Alexander Severus became emperor when his cousin Elagabalus was assassinated.

135 Aurelian was Roman emperor during the Crisis of the Third Century. He won an unprecedented series of military victories and reunited the Roman Empire.

Those capabilities of credible valor were in Charles V; those of justice were critical in Philip II; those of religion were glorious in Philip III; those of government and administration were heroic in Philip IV the Great; and all together, they are connatural in the Perfect King.

A king must never vacate his throne of greatness, because his nature requires an outlet and Heaven demands accountability for his talents; when one occasion ceases, he must pass on to another. This rule was well known to Julius Caesar, the man of the most capable and fruitful heart. When he had no more provinces to subdue, he undertook to level the mountains. Having given laws to men, he tried to give them rivers and seas. After having restored order to the globe, he set about reforming time.[136] Well pondered the profound Gaius Veleius[137] when he said that "in finishing his military conquests, he finished himself. And death, which spared him in so many years of dangerous war, found him after only five months of rest."

They call on each other's deeds and facilitate each other's executions.[138] This is how they aided Suleiman,[139] who aged in their company for forty years, creating a flourishing empire. The first year they secured Egypt, and when he

---

136   "He set about reforming time." This is a reference to the Julian Calendar.

137   Gaius Veleius, often referred to simply as Catullus, was a Latin poet of the late Roman Republic who wrote chiefly in the neoteric style of poetry, focusing on personal life rather than classical heroes. His surviving works are still read widely and continue to influence poetry and other forms of art.

138   The different capabilities of a king aid each other by demanding of each other and helping each other execute the king's talents.

139   Suleiman the Magnificent was Sultan of the Ottoman Empire for forty-six years and undertook bold military campaigns that enlarged his realm and oversaw the development of what came to be regarded as the most characteristic achievements of Ottoman civilization in the fields of law, literature, art, and architecture.

was not content with his victory in the Siege of Rhodes, they later longed for that of Malta;[140] but he could not fully occupy the island because his power lacked the assistance of a great mind.[141] Yet his seraglios[142] were his conquered kingdoms, and his exhibits were his well-deserved triumphs. He truly was a monarch of good taste!

When a king begins to engage his capabilities, he should not find himself without new heroic occupations. In this way, the Caesar of the Spaniards, Charles,[143] alternated between them; from humiliating the heretics, he went on to confront the Turks; from captivating one king to chasing away another. And the conquests of Africa were his vacations from the conquests of Europe.

This is the worthy use of these royal treasures. Badly used were those of Nero and Caligula, and much was achieved with those of the great Aragonese King, Don Jaime I.

---

140 A reference to the Siege of Malta, which saw the Christians, outnumbered six to one, withstand the Ottomans in a siege of more than four months and endure the bombardment of over 130,000 cannonballs.

141 Here, Gracián says that Suleiman's power was hindered by his lack of great generals. "Lacked the assistance of a great mind" is a reference to Generals Don García Álvarez de Toledo and Grandmaster Jean Parisot de Valette, who outmaneuvered the Ottoman army and led the outnumbered Christians to victory.

142 Seraglio is a Muslim palace.

143 A reference to Charles V the Holy Roman Emperor.

-VI-
A King of Sound Administration

A responsible monarch acts discreetly, spends prudently, and repays loans successfully. The kings of Portugal were magnificently successful in this, obtaining income and honors at the same time.

Like Fernando, the Perfect King must be sagacious and spare useless vain endeavors, which are not of profit but of theme and affectation. The attachment to vassals and treasures, such as those of the Pedros of Castilla and Aragón, originates more from stubborn emulation than from convenience or prudence, and the end result of such enterprises is nothing other than the devastation of both king and kingdom.

To desire fame and notoriety is to choose between a poor woman and a sterile one; two extremes of which a prince can only be uselessly proud of.

Henry IV of France administered to his kingdom a thousand paternal comforts, and, having realized their intrinsic value, he put his adherents before himself. A king ensures the health of his kingdom by purging himself of the unnecessary and superfluous and by giving his kingdom a sense of destiny, because in the absence of both self-governance and conquests, republics suffer from internal seditions. A great aphorism was always to make an antidote of the poison.

It was idleness that gnawed away at the continued happiness of Spain, and a perennial source of vices that destroyed Rome. There is no greater enemy than not having enemies. And so, when a king has no external adversaries, he must look within himself for evils to defeat. Metellus[144] made a strong statement of courage with his victory over Carthage,[145] and an even greater statement by learning to live with the trauma of his harmful experience years later.[146] The Ottomans did not usually live without war, and by changing enemies, they stimulated their courage with intermissions and their experiences by forgetting them, always keeping their militia flourishing.

Military power is the basis of reputation: an unarmed prince is a dead lion, whom even the hares insult.

Fernando did not disband his squadrons after having ended the war in Granada; here, the carelessness of Rodrigo served him as a lesson, and after throwing out of Spain the last remnants of Islam, he made his army a living wall to protect his kingdoms.

He knew how to estimate and administer his great power; having his finger on the pulse of his forces, he knew how to use them; he had his enemies in his sights and knew how to

---

144 Lucius Metellus, consul and dictator of Rome.
145 Metellus defeated the much larger Carthaginian Army and their thirteen generals at the Battle of Panormus.
146 A reference to the fire that destroyed the Temple of Vesta and threatened to destroy the Palladium and other sacred objects. When Metellus saw the fire spreading, he, without hesitating, threw himself into the flames to save Rome's artifacts. However, his eyes were badly injured by the intense heat, and he went blind. Here, Gracián says that when he could no longer conquer the enemies of Rome, he used his courage to conquer himself and find the will to continue living.

prevent them; by taking the Spaniards to foreign provinces, he transformed them into lions; by always attacking the French, he always defeated them, and he never gave place to the prevention of victory. He understood nations and humanity and gave them each their own food.

But the eminence of this great king was always waging war with muted gunpowder. That is, without the dangerous and vain noises of arming; without company riots that warn the opponents, irritate those who remain neutral, and wake up everyone. Without playing landowner, he took a place in Africa, a kingdom in Spain, an island in the ocean, a city in Italy, and all this with the alacrity of a lion. Like him, the Perfect King must be a man who knows the proper occasion for arms, the perfect season for business, and the proper timing of everything.

A king of prudent administration is equivalent to the most important armies of his kingdom.

A famously celebrated political question is whether the king should be present in one center and everywhere by power and by news or whether, like the sun, he should move around the whole horizon of his empire, administering, illustrating, influencing, and vivifying everywhere. There are effective arguments and accredited examples for each opinion; let us visit each of them.

All the great kings who did great things attended to their enterprises in person. Thus, the great Alexander in ten years raided Greece, subdued Persia, subdued Scythia, tamed India, and conquered the East, filling the world with terror and posterity with fame. The great Caesar achieved numerous triumphs: he conquered Gaul and subjugated the French, conquered Britannia, confronted Germania, defeated the African Juba, humiliated Pharnaces II of Pontus, and extinguished the relics of General Pompey. The famous Hannibal was only twenty years old when he bested Rome, defeating five generals and three Roman consuls in the Siege of Saguntum and ninety thousand Roman senators in the battle of Cannae. The magnanimous Augustus happily ended five civil wars and subdued twelve barbarian nations, and all the nations of the world sent him their ambassadors and presents. Trajan passed the limits of the Empire and conquered the other side of the Tigris and Euphrates Rivers. Charlemagne established his throne and girded his venerable gray hair with three crowns, becoming King of the Franks, King of the Lombards, and the Holy Roman Emperor. Mohammad conquered two empires, twelve kingdoms, and more than two hundred cities. The Great Conqueror Don Jaime I started and won thirty pitched battles. Quingui overwhelmed nine kingdoms and destroyed many others. Otto the Great fought thirty years, triumphing over the princes of Germany, Bohemia, Hungary, and the Berengarius in Italy. He despoiled all of Asia and, in three years, devastated Albania, Iberia, Armenia, Persia, Mesopotamia, and Egypt. Boleslaus of Poland defeated the Saxons and Kashubians, conquered Pomerania, and embarrassed Boleslaus, the King of Bohemia.

Mahomet, the Great Mughal, terrorized Asia with eight hundred thousand combatants and established his empire between the two rivers, the Indus and Ganges.

The victorious Don Alonso Enríquez, the first king of Portugal, spent sixty years fighting against the Moors, defeating, over several encounters, eight kings and beheading seven. Ismael Sophi conquered Persia, Mesopotamia, Media, Cappadocia, Iberia, Armenia, and Albania. The Holy Emperor Charles V humiliated the greatest kings that the world has ever had: he captivated the prince of France, caused the Turks to faint, imprisoned the prince of Mexico, stripped the Inca, and dismantled the prince of Tunisia, among others. But to whom all admiration is paid is to the great Semiramis, who founded Babylon: not content with the vast monarchy of Assyria, she conquered Egypt, undertook India, and, leading a million people with two thousand ships, defeated King Staurobates on the waters of the Indus River; afterwards, while dressing her hair, they gave her news that Babylon had rebelled and, without finishing the dressing, she went, saw, and conquered.

So all the hero kings—those who accomplished great deeds—personally led their armies. There is a political proverb among the warlike Ottomans: "Victory is not achieved where the Great Lord is not found."

For soldiers, to see their king is to be rewarded and his presence is worth another army. With only one hundred men and his royal valor, the great King Pedro of Aragón[147] went to oppose King Philip of France, who was entering Catalonia with sixteen thousand in calvary, seventeen thousand crossbowmen, six hundred knights, all of lineage, one hundred thousand well armed infantrymen, fifty thousand soldiers, and one hundred ships.[148] Only Don Pedro was enough to stop the French fury at that time, and, with moderate support, he finished King Philip and, afterwards, all of his army. Sardanapalus lost his golden monarchy because he was spinning on the infamous platforms of his harlots and died in an orgy of self-destruction; and Darius perished because of his extravagances; when he went out to resist Alexander, though he knew he could not, it was with spears of gold and chari-

---

147 **King Pedro III of Aragón was the son of King Jaime I, the Conqueror.**

148 **A reference to the Aragonese Crusade, which was a military venture by the Kingdom of France and Pope Martin IV. Outnumbering the Aragonese, the French saw some successes on land, but King Pedro's admiral, Roger de Lauria, commanding the Aragonese Navy, won control of the sea, and the badly attrited French army was forced to retreat in the fall of 1285.**

ots of ivory. For not wanting to lose a flower from one of his gardens, Gallienus lost twenty provinces and suffered thirty tyrants to rise up against him.

Rodrigo was lost first in delightful peace and then in battle. The negligent Constantine XI let himself be surrounded by pleasures in his court and his palace, and when he did not want to go out to look for an enemy, the enemy came to look for him in Constantinople.[149]

Those famous kings Augustus, Trajan, and Theodosius returned victorious to their Rome, viewed as living theaters of triumph, while Tiberius, Nero, Caligula, Domitian, and Elagabalus were seen as the quagmires of their delights.

Happiness before all necessary movements are achieved is false security, while unnecessary movements lead to ruin. The Portuguese Don Sebastian died a victim of his own tragedies, and his recklessness made other kings more than sane. Some lose their kingdoms to audacity, while others lose them to punishment.

On the contrary, others say that the office of a king is to command, not to execute, and thus his sphere is the canopy, not the tent; the head is so important that to keep it even brutes expose their whole body piece by piece. Who would support that a king expose his life, kingdom, and honor to the risk of fate after so many examples of ancient and modern chastisements? Of an Emperor Valerian,[150] who was made a footstool at the feet of the Barbarian Shapur; of the Sultan Bayezid, who was made a captive of Tamerlane

---
149   A reference to the fall of Constantinople.

150   Valerian is known as the first Roman emperor to have been taken captive in battle. He was captured by the Persian emperor Shapur I after the Battle of Edessa, causing shock and instability throughout the Roman Empire. During his captivity, Valerian was used as a human footstool when Shapur would mount his horse.

and put in a golden cage, a punishment proportionate to his fierceness; of a wretched Ladislaus, King of Poland, who was mocked by fortune, ill-advised by his own, victoriously vanquished, and made an anvil of the ottomans; after Don Alfonso of Aragón died in Fraga,[151] when no enemy had ever boasted of having seen an Aragonese king defeated and dead; after a King Francis of France was called the Great, only to be held as Spain's greatest captive; of a Sebastian, the sun that at dawn was eclipsed by the African moons.[152]

Caesar fought well to be emperor, and Valerian fought badly to stop being emperor. Almanzor[153] conquered Spain by his captains and preserved Africa by himself. Emperor Charles V achieved more victories absent from his armies than present. Some kings found themselves in battles to raise their monarchies; but, already established, it is not prudent to risk everything. The very happy King Manuel of Portugal never went seeking victories in Africa and Asia; they came to him and entered through his gates, and the East came to prostrate itself at his feet.

But between these two extremes, the Perfect King must emulate Fernando and find the middle ground: neither always walking like Hadrian nor always loafing like Gallienus.

---

151   King Alfonso I of Aragón, called the Warrior. He was known for his great military successes against Islam, having conquered Zaragoza, Ejea, Tudela, Calatayud, Borja, Tarazona, Daroca, and Monreal del Campo. He died in the Battle of Fraga, fighting against the Muslims.

152   A reference to King Sebastian of Portugal invading North Africa and dying in battle.

153   See footnote 123.

-VII-
A King of Discernment

The Catholic Fernando did not fix his court in any of the cities of Spain, either because he did not consider his monarchy definite, always aspiring for more, or because of a profound opinion of not making one nation the head and another the feet. A point of so much attention that, for this very reason, the political kings of China indicated two cities, Panjin and Nanjing, as the seats of their greatness, alternating stays in accordance with the inclemencies of the times, as security for their vassals, and equalizing favors and burdens between them.

In all monarchies, there was always a royal center of command. Some cities were chosen because the monarchy began in them. Thus, Rome was the head of its great empire and then of the whole world, the crowned emporium of all its riches, delights, greatness, and wonders; the universal mother of nations, which came to have five million souls. Others were so by choice, attending to the conveniences of either politics or the economy, as in the case of Constantinople, first for the Christian empire, then for the Ottoman, qualifying as the first choice of both for being an imperial city located in the most perfect place of the world: in terms of Europe and Asia, dominating the seas; queen of the cities of Europe, for the beauty of its site, comforts of its port, greatness of its buildings, richness of its solace, abundance of supplies, and court of the Grand Turk.

The great Court of Nineveh was born in the first empire of the world, which was that of the Assyrians, and grew so much that it took three days' journey to walk its entirety, according to Divine History. It competed with Babylon with its hundred bronze gates, walls of fifty cubits in latitude and more than two hundred in altitude, and its three thousand towers. Semiramis fabricated it; Nebuchadnezzar enlarged it, so much so that Aristotle said, "it feels like an eternity trying to see only a small part of it." But, forgetting the courts of the already forgotten empires, Paris deserved to be the seat of the most Christian kings more than a thousand years ago, for the supply of its land, with more than twelve thousand populations within ten leagues of contour, and even today it is the largest city in Christendom. London, England, for the pleasantness of its countryside and for the navigability of the Thames, its river; Vienna, in Germany,[154] for its strength and its faithfulness; Stockholm, in Sweden, for the marvelousness of its lake and the frequency of its port; Krakow, in Poland, famous for its schools and strong for its castles; Moscow, in Moscovia, for its healthy land, where the plague never found entrance, so populated that it is counted among the four great cities of Europe. Tabriz, in Persia, crowned with gardens, watered by a thousand fountains, bathed in salubrious air, and supplied with all kinds of delicacies. Khanbaliq,[155] the winter capital of the Yuan Dynasty, has such great commerce that a thousand carts of silk from China enter it every year and it surpasses all other cities in the magnificence of its palace; Samarkand, in the Moghuls,[156] first enriched with the spoils of all Asia and

---
154 Modern day Austria.
155 Modern day Beijing.
156 Modern day Uzbekistan.

of such greatness that there used to be in it sixty thousand horses; the Barbary Coast, displaying the most beautiful and most populous of all Africa, girded and penetrated by the sea, a royal emporium of letters and riches.

Fernando left this choice to the happiness of his successors, who, once the monarchy was established, chose Madrid, because it was the center of Spain and because of its healthy terrain.

To the enterprises outside of Spain, which were not the least glorious, he attended, if not by his presence, by his direction, entrusted to famous caudillos, prudent viceroys, attentive ambassadors raised in his school, and graduates of his choice.

This great job of reigning cannot be exercised alone: it must be communicated to the entire series of ministers, who are immediate kings. What does it matter that the king himself is excellent if his assistants discredit him? Stenkil of Sweden was an illustrious king, but his unworthy viceroys obscured him. Charles d'Anjou made royal garments of his virtues, but he was abhorred for the iniquity of his ministers until he lost the fertile kingdom of Sicily on that memorable afternoon.[157]

The errors or the successes of a king's ministers will fall on his head; there were inferior kings, not at all advantaged by their personal capacities, who were greatly celebrated for the eminence of their ministers. The genius of General Narses and Belisarius[158] made Emperor Justinian immortal;

---

157 A reference to the Sicillian Vespers of 1282, where the Sicilians massacred the French and began their revolt against Charles with the help of King Pedro III of Aragón, son of King Jaime I of Aragón, the Conqueror.

158 Narses and Belisarius were great generals who served under Emperor Justinian during the Roman reconquest.

Theophilus and Tribonian,[159] with their togas, made him a sage; and, conversely, there were kings eminent themselves for their greatness but remembered poorly for their inferior instruments of reign.

The illustrious Margaret,[160] superiorly qualified, deserved by her person to be queen of Denmark, Norway, and Sweden; but her ministers were undeserving, and she lost the kingdoms. And it is a pity that the inestimable royal reputation of a maximum Charles[161] in Spain perishes not for his faults, which he did not have, but for those of his greedy governors. The Perfect King must be a king of great discernment and, therefore, a king of great choice. Don Enrique III of Castilla (who prided himself on being a great governor, and indeed he was) greatly appreciated his outstanding ministers, both of militia and government, because he knew their importance.

King Philip II, the Prudent, always kept them with artificial dependence, tempering their many hopes with some fruition, which is the art of knowing how to lead the ministers: how to make them and keep them.

---

159   Theophilus and Tribonian supervised the revision of the legal code for Emperor Justinian and the Byzantine Empire.

160   Margaret I was Queen Regnant of Denmark, Norway, and Sweden (which included Finland) and the founder of the Kalmar Union, which joined the Scandinavian kingdoms together for over a century. She was known as a wise, energetic, and capable leader who governed with farsighted tact and caution, earning the nickname "the Semiramis of the North." She was also known by her subjects as "Lady King," which became widely used in recognition of her capabilities. She is considered the first great ruling queen in European history.

161   A reference to the Holy Roman Emperor Charles V, also known as King Charles I of Spain.

Some attribute having good ministers to the luck of a king, but it is more a matter of prudence, of knowing how to choose them, or of science, of knowing how to make them.

Not only does a wise king choose the best from among them, but he also makes them, forms them, and trains them. The king does not ask if they are astute, because if they are, he will already know.

A political king forms them into politicians. Louis XI of France infused them with greatness, even the men of a more common constitution, which he judged rightly with the veracity of his political spirit. Oh, his intelligence in discovering, his reflexes in preventing, his skill in negotiating, and his ingenuity in proceeding!

A warrior king, valiant and exercised in weapons, brings out of them great warriors; it was a seminary of distinguished captains in the tent of the Emperor Charles V. He worked great things for himself and greater things for them; his extraordinary skill was attached to them and assisted them.

So, the politician Louis makes them politicians; the battler Don Jaime I of Aragón, valiant; the wise Charles of France, wise; the great governor Enrique of Castilla, great governors; the saintly Fernando III, pious; the prudent Philip, prudent; and the just Don Jaime II, just.

And the great Philip IV of Spain, because he is everything, has as a minister, or, rather, an arch-minister: His Excellency, Don Gaspar de Guzman, Count-Duke of Olivares, eminent in everything, the Great Minister of the Great Monarch.[162]

---

162 Later on in his life, Gracián's opinion of the Count-Duke, Gaspar de Guzman, would sour when the Count had his patron and friend, the Duke of Nochera, Don Francisco María Carrafa, whom he served as confessor during the Catalonian revolt, falsely charged with conspiring with the French and imprisoned, where he would later die.

Truly a giant of a hundred arms, of a hundred understandings, and of a hundred prudences. No doubt Heaven foresaw for the greatest risks of this Catholic Monarchy the greatest men. And the conspiracy of the whole world against it has been for naught but ensuring that its royal and ducal virtues would come out to the universal light of the whole world and of all the centuries.

But what helped Fernando the most to become a consummate prince of virtue and courage were the enlightened and heroic qualities of the never sufficiently praised Queen Isabella, his Catholic Queen, that great princess who, though a woman, exceeded the limits of manhood.

The good and prudent woman brings much good, and the imprudent one, much evil. Mothers, out of respect, wives, out of love, do much that affect a king. The wise and sane Mesa, in the time she lived, did not cover up but confronted the monstrosities of Elagabalus, her grandson. The saintly Empress Helena engendered Christianity and all virtue to her son, the great emperor Constantine. While his religious mother lived, Frederick became emperor. Much of the heroic holiness of Louis IX of France is due to the teachings of the Spaniard Doña Blanca, his great mother. The Aragonese saint Doña Isabel, immortal queen of Portugal, was an oracle of virtue and peace between King Don Denis I, called the Fabricator,[163] her husband, and Prince Don Alfonso, called the Brave, her son. With her religious discipline, she defeated all military discipline, and with her piety, she broke up the armed squads of a father against a son and of a son against a father, cross against cross, kingdom threatening kingdom. Our inestimable queen and lady, Margarita of Austria, greater wealth of Spain, whose holy memory is

---
163 King Denis ordered the construction of numerous castles and created new towns, hence the moniker "the Fabricator" (Spanish: *el Fabricador*).

always fresh by her continuous weeping, made her husband more holy and filled the world with Catholic successions of Faith, columns of Religion, and suns of Christianity.

Blessed is the king whom a prudent and holy mother brings a second time to the light of virtue and, as a Christian emissary, forms and informs him!

However, the intense love of a wife tends to predominate more in the will of a king than the reverential love of a mother; many were enlightened by their queens, and many were tarnished by them. This difference was seen in King Don Juan I of Aragón, whose first wife made him kind to his vassals, and his second, abhorrent.

Passions commonly reign in women in such a way that they leave no room for counsel, for waiting, for prudence, or for the essential parts of government, and with their power, their tyranny increases tyranny. But she who is of a nature that Heaven has corrected is wise and prudent, and extremely so, and ordinarily, the more manly ones are naturally prudent also.

A king, once assured of the good capacity of his queen, should give her a place as co-ruler but always with moderation. King Don Ramiro of León was worth two, aided by the prudence and courage of Queen Urraca,[164] his wife, and much more was King Don Juan II of Aragón with Queen Juana,[165] both dividing their work: while the king led the armies in one kingdom, the queen held courts in the other

---

164 King Ramiro II of León and Queen Urraca Sánchez of Pamplona. King Ramiro is remembered as an excellent military commander, who expanded his territories south to such a remarkable extent that the Moors referred to him as "the Devil" because of his ferocity and fervor in battle. His queen, Urraca, was known for her prudence, modesty, and acumen.

165 See footnote 23.

and, like a shining moon, made up for the absences of the well busy king.

The advice of a woman is not much, but sometimes it is of critical importance; all was lost by King Don Juan, the last king of Navarre, by not embracing it; perhaps he would have stayed king if he listened to the advice of the woman who made him king.[166]

It is good for a king to celebrate his command of all, but to yield to reason in all, and more so in a wise and holy queen.

A prudent, sane, and sagacious sister can also well enter in place of a wife or mother. King Don Enrique I of Castilla was aided by his sister, the enlightened queen of León, Doña Berenguela,[167] who, while she assisted him, enjoyed the tranquility of Castilla. In Spain, prudent females have always been as capable as men, and in the house of Austria, they have always been esteemed and employed.

The Catholic queen, Doña Isabel, was rare and singular among all, with such great capacity that even next to

---

166 John III was a French nobleman who became King of Navarre through marriage with Queen Catherine.

167 Queen Berenguela, known as the Great, was Spain's most capable queen and served as advisor to not only her brother but also to her son, the saint, King Fernando III of Castilla. When her brother, King Enriquez died, she declared herself heir of his kingdom, made herself queen, and quickly surrendered the throne to Fernando, so his father, King Alfonso, whom she considered to have nefarious intentions, could not claim it. She remained Fernando's closest advisor, guiding policy, negotiating, and ruling on his behalf for the rest of her life. She was responsible for the reunification of Castilla and León under her son's authority, supported his efforts in the Reconquista, and even influenced his choice of wife, Elisabeth of Swabia. She is regarded as the wisest, most capable, and most virtuous Spanish queen by the chroniclers of history.

Fernando, her great king, she was not only able to make herself known but to shine.

And so, the Perfect King must qualify with proof and show himself, first by choosing and then by esteeming. Using each of the two to create a golden century and a very happy reign, and even more so when paired together.

-VIII-

The Phoenix of Kings

A king must go where few have gone—to the extremities of action—in order to make his government a dependency, to make the monarchy know that it needs him and not the other way around, so that the same people who would drive him away with their ingratitude will urge him with their entreaties and consider it a greater evil to lack his wise opinions than to submit to his indignant prudence.

Few princes reach this glory; usually they are more detested than desired; if Don Sancho of Castilla deserved the moniker "the Strong," it was more for the hope that he inspired than for his victories in battle. Titus could not reach the six good years[168] but was still seen as exemplary. Some were snatched away before malice could change their good judgment.[169]

Variety is the mother of taste and, at least, of relief and, at most, of fortune. A change in luck has always been plausible, and many do not realize that the ups and downs of one instance reverberate into other instances and unto other successors.

---
168   Similar to the concept of a 5-year plan, it is believed that a ruler needs 6 years to implement real change. Unfortunately, Titus died of a fever only 3 years into being emperor.
169   "Some were snatched away" is a reference to the assassination of King Sancho and the death of Emperor Titus.

Like Fernando, the Perfect King must be privileged in universality, a phoenix of command that is reborn with unique applause. When Fernando returned to Castilla with a triumph of reputation, he was praised for being a master of diplomacy, and it was said of the Catholic King that the remedy of his monarchy, if it should decline, was none other than for the king to rise again and restore it.

Established, a king must master time and occasion, and perfect them in every kind of adornment, culture, and policy.

Romulus founded the Roman Republic but did not have time to give perfection her place, which led to his fraternal punishment and the deceitful Roman Senate as a consequential reward;[170] this obligation remained for his successors and is a reminder of what is not the least important rule of politics: leaving your successor gloriously committed to heroic conquests and not political quagmire. In this way, Suleiman the Magnificent, an inexperienced young man, awoke and, with the rebellion of the Mamelukes, transformed himself from a meek lamb just beginning to reign into his army's most ferocious lion.

Ultimately, Romulus' successor, Numa, entered and instituted religion, although false, as the foundation of all government. He invented gods and introduced worship, priests, and sacrifices. He was succeeded by Tullus Hostilius, who put into being the militia, adding discipline to courage. Then Ancus Marcius adorned the city with buildings, walls, and bridges and founded the colonies. After him, Priscus authorized the royal majesty and those of the magistrates with laws and insignia. Lastly, Servius Tullius established the revenues of the Republic, the taxes and levies, which, if

---
170 "His fraternal punishment and the deceitful Roman Senate as a consequential reward" is a reference to the murder of Emperor Romulus by members of the Roman Senate and the political power the Senate subsequently attained.

moderate, are the nerves of its conservation and, if excessive, of its ruin. So Romulus forms the monarchy, and the others advance and perfect it.

What all these did in the monarchy of Rome, Fernando did in the monarchy of Spain and a Perfect King must also do in his monarchy. He must make it religious by purging it of infidels and by exalting the sacred and vigilant wisdom of the Holy Scriptures. He must make it courageous, making a sudden fear of his power known to foreign nations with his efforts; majestic, by putting in place his royal authority. Rich, not with tribute but with perennial fleets, rivers of gold, silver, pearls, and other riches that enter every year from afar. Ingenious, by knowing how to discover men who are learned and distinguished in human and divine letters and raising them up to be ministers; and, finally, happy in every kind of perfection and culture. So that, with much reason, his descendants, making courtesy of his portraits, will add, "to this one, we owe everything."

When his successes are well known and certain, he must never be content with himself. He must never be satisfied with his interior and public approval; a great king must examine himself assiduously; he must police himself without mercy.

Many ask, "if it is so difficult for a man to rightly judge himself, how will a king do it?" To accurately estimate oneself is not permitted by one's own fondness; and to see oneself in others is equally difficult due to transcendental adulation. And so, a king has no mirror, but here, he allows criticism to enter… if he is wise.

Prince Germanicus dismounted and, thus, went in search of the truth through the dispassionate legions of his soldiers. Perhaps he listened to praise with enjoyment and perhaps the opposite, with disappointment.

Our Holy Roman Emperor Charles V made use of criticism as a spy on his reputation and explored the spirits of his men with her incautious freedom. Neither hatred nor flattery are faithful crystals; they adulterate what is found in truth; the former will say that virtues are really vices, while the latter, that vices are really virtues.

Lost in the hunt, Francis I of France, since then Great, spent nights in the house of simplicity and even among some villains until the sun of truth dawned on him and the most discreet king repeated, "If those around me are mute, I lose even if I win." But of course.

From some simpletons and fools, she (criticism) has made very prudent kings, oracles of the truth who alone speak it. Because they embraced her, they have the courage to relate without suspicion to what others say in front of them and without hesitation. This was King Fernando's relevant subtlety and the crown of his policy; and it should be the same for all discreet kings.

He died at sixty-four years of precious age, and after forty years of a happy reign. Great happiness for a monarchy when its kings die old! He lived briefly in fruition and eternally in desire. The day Fernando and his great grandson, Charles V, died, all Christendom cried and all infidelity rejoiced; times again turned dark the day Selim and his son, the Magnificent, perished.[171]

But Fernando did not die, because famous men never do. Fame always goes to extremes; and there is no mediocrity in kings. They are known either as very good or very bad; and just as there are some glorious and distinct prodigies, so too are there detestable monsters. Some are the foundation of a

---
171 A reference to Selim I, known as the Resolute, and his son, Suleiman the Magnificent.

monarchy and cause it to rise; others are stumbling blocks that cause it to fall: kings of horror, of scandal, of infamy, whose memory is eternalized in the bronzes of tradition. Some put an end to the Monarchy, as Constantine XI did to that of Greece; others, to its prosperity, as Childeric did to that of Clovis; and others, to its religion, as did Henry VIII of England. The kingdom of Israel began to decline under Rehoboam for his imprudence; and under Gallienus, the Roman Empire, for his laziness; with Andronikos I Komnenos, the Greek, for his inadvertence. The monarchy of the Assyrians perished under Sardanapalus for his decadence; under Astyages, that of the Medians, for his tyranny; under Darius, that of the Persians, for his carelessness; with Rodrigo, that of the Goths, for his lewdness. The falsehoods of Tiberius, the iniquity of Caligula, the solidity of Claudius, the tyranny of Nero, the lust of Elagabalus, the insensitivity of Gallienus, the ineptitude of Charles the Frenchman, the cruelty of Pedro the Castilian, and the laziness of Sancho the Portuguese will all last forever. The abomination of Henry IV the German, the infamy of Mauregatus the Usurper of Asturias, the blindness of Henry VIII. A king should always tremble at the thought of being added to such a horrible list of men.

But a Perfect King will dwell in an august theater with the reputation of honor, of heroism, of brilliance, and in it, various choirs will sing his praises, according to his eminences and distinctions, and in all of them he will be admired as the Catholic Fernando was, with transcendent applause: in the theater of a sacred Catholic piety, with Emperor Theodosius, King Henrique of Portugal, and Rudolf I of Germany; between the three Fernandos, the I of León, the II of Aragón, and the III of Castilla, the first of these who was also Emperor of all Spain; with the great Goth, King Wamba, and King Pelayo who established Christian Asturias; with Philip III of Spain; with King Clovis, Charlemagne, and

Louis IX of France; with Stephen I of Hungary, Henry I of Sweden, Olaus I of Norway, and Casimir of Poland.

In the theater of valor, with the greatest Emperor, Julius Caesar, with King Don Jaime, the Conqueror of Aragón, with the Holy Roman Emperor, Charles V, with Suleiman the Magnificent and his brave son Selim I, and Henry IV of France; with the great Alexander, Constantine I, Charlemagne, Alfonso VIII of Castilla, and Philip IV of Spain. In the theater of the wise and sagacious, between Ismael Sofi, Charles V of France, Albert I of Austria, and Don Sancho IV of Navarre. Among the diplomats, between Louis XI of France, Stephanus Bator of Poland, and Matthias Corvinus of Hungary. With the prudent, between an Emperor Justinian, Maximilian I, Gustav I of Sweden, and Philip II of Spain. Among the magnanimous, between Ninus I of Assyria, Xerxes I of Persia, Octavian Augustus, and King Don Alfonso of Naples. With those who are well-regarded, among Hispán, who gave Spain his surname; Emperor Titus, the most accomplished and benevolent of men: eloquent, warlike, and moderate in his desires, he was called "the love and the delight of the human race"; the Holy Roman Emperor Otto III, called "the miracle of the world"; and Don Sancho the Desired. In that of the most ideal, those chosen and well-suited for the most arduous of circumstances, among an Emperor Numa Pompilius, Philip the Macedon, Antoninus Pius, and Don Manuel of Portugal. Among the just, between Antiochus III, known as the Great, who retracted all the injustices of his empire; Seleucus I, the Macedonian, who esteemed justice more than his own eyes; with Emperor Aurelian and Emperor Nerva, who punished traitors and the ungrateful; with Don Jaime II of Aragón, called the Just; and Don Alfonso XI of Castilla, the Avenger. And finally, in all the catalogs of applause and fame, where we find our singular Fernando, the Catholic: courageous, magnanimous, political, prudent, wise, beloved, just, benevolent, and a universal hero.

This treatise, which I consider an immortal crown of mine, is a rough copy, paying homage to the one who was the most perfect paragon of monarchs and whom all who aspire to be a Perfect King should imitate. The last king of the Goths by male line, but the first in the world by his virtues, whose greatest success, among so many, was to have exalted the name of the Most High through Heaven's divine choice of Catholic Spain.

Like Fernando, may the Perfect King be a House that God exalts, and may he exalt it with his Church to end the discord that is as old as cruelty between the emperors and the sacred Pontiffs; may he be the beginning of peace and order in his kingdom. A House in which, after his reign, the Church of the Lord will not know what schisms are, because he never knew them. A House that returns the Supreme Christ of Nazareth to his throne, as head of the Church and our souls, and maintains his supreme authority. A House that is raised by God to be the wall of Christianity against the perversion and secularism of this dark world. A House that God strengthens to be a hammer against the heretics and crush the enemies of Christ. A House that God forms to be a very rich mine of saints, emperors, empresses, kings, queens, and archdukes. A House that God extends throughout the whole roundness of the earth to spread throughout it his Holy Faith and Gospel. A House that God chooses according to his law of grace as well as according to that of Abraham in the written law; all glory to the God of Asturia, the God of Rudolf, Philip, and Fernando.

May this treatise then be the august choice of instruction for a Christian prince who desires to be the Perfect King and the perfect representation of Christian zeal and great power, the guardian of prudent government and dilator of the most ideal monarchy, and may Heaven make him universal. Amen.

Works by Baltasar Gracián

El Héroe (1637)

El Político (1640)

El Arte de Ingenio (1642)

El Discreto (1646)

El Oráculo Manual y Arte de Prudencia (1647)

El Comulgatorio (1655)

El Criticón (1651–1657)

About the Translator

Website: https://StVitus.Dance
Email: TheMikeSanPedro@gmail.com

www.ingramcontent.com/pod-product-compliance
Lightning Source LLC
Chambersburg PA
CBHW040251090526
44586CB00041B/2782